Ghosts of Delaware

Mark Sarro & Gerard J. Medvec

Schiffer Publishing Ltd ®

4880 Lower Valley Road • Atglen, PA 19310

Other Schiffer Books By The Author:

Ghosts of West Chester, **Pennsylvania**
ISBN 978-0-7643-2996-8 $14.99
Haunted Gettysburg
ISBN 978-0-7643-3310-1 $19.99

Design by Danielle D. Farmer
Type set in Argenta/Bauhaus Lt, Md BT

ISBN: 978-0-7643-4139-7
Printed in The United States

Schiffer Books are available at special discounts for bulk purchases for sales promotions or premiums. Special editions, including personalized covers, corporate imprints, and excerpts can be created in large quantities for special needs. For more information contact the publisher:

Published by Schiffer Publishing, Ltd.
4880 Lower Valley Road
Atglen, PA 19310
Phone: (610) 593-1777; Fax: (610) 593-2002
E-mail: Info@schifferbooks.com

For the largest selection of fine reference books on this and related subjects, please visit our website at **www.schifferbooks.com**
We are always looking for people to write books on new and related subjects. If you have an idea for a book, please contact us at proposals@schifferbooks.com

This book may be purchased from the publisher.
Please try your bookstore first.
You may write for a free catalog.

In Europe, Schiffer books are distributed by
Bushwood Books
6 Marksbury Ave.
Kew Gardens
Surrey TW9 4JF England
Phone: 44 (0) 20 8392 8585; Fax: 44 (0) 20 8392 9876
E-mail: info@bushwoodbooks.co.uk
Website: www.bushwoodbooks.co.uk

Dedication

MARK'S DEDICATION

This book is for my mother, Joyce, and my grandmother, Mary; without them I would have never made it this far. Their continued love and support has helped to make me the man that I am today.

GERRY'S DEDICATION

This book is for my beautiful wife, Joyce, my best friend, the world's greatest meatball maker and a phenomenal front-line editor. Of course, she is much more than all of that – she is *the* soul mate, *my* soul mate.

Acknowledgments

MARK'S ACKNOWLEDGMENTS

I want to thank Dinah Roseberry at Schiffer Publishing for her continued support over the years. Thank you for keeping this dream alive. Mary Gasparo, a friend and colleague who always has my back in the paranormal or otherwise. Bob Meyers and Carol Starr, CCPRS – would not have had the longevity and continued success without contributions and support from both of you. Uber Radio Network, for giving me a voice to be heard again. MK Omega, the best group of musicians I have ever had the pleasure of playing with. My family: Nikki, Kimberly, and Mom; Dad, Luke, Sherri, and my nephews, Steven and Derrick. Last but not least, my co-author Gerry Medvec. You made this book possible! Thanks for the inspiration!

GERRY'S ACKNOWLEDGMENTS

I never thought the day would dawn when I'd have to ask myself, "Who would I put in the acknowledgments of my first book?" But today's the day.

Thanks to my fantastic and amazing daughters, Sabrina and Marissa, for tolerating Dad on his journeys into altered-states. And girls, I apologize for forgetting which one is amazing and which one fantastic. Thanks to my sons, Landru and Sagan, for growing up so easily, and for becoming trustworthy men. Thanks to my dear friends, Jo Ellen Frymiare, Rraine Parodi, Jane Bunting, and my spirit friend, Roberta Rausch, for not judging me when discussing my paranormal plights, and for your love, support, and training on how to deal with women. All of you helped me be a better man.

Thanks again to my Joyce for raising such wonderful children, now my stepchildren. Sherri, Mark, and Luke are some of the nicest people I've ever met. It is an honor to know you all.

Thanks especially to my co-author/stepson, Mark, the genie in my lamp. Buddy, you made my authorship wish come true.

The spirit realm must also be given gratitude. Without its infinite antics, there would be no book.

Contents

Foreword

~Mark Sarro

It only seems appropriate that eventually I would have an opportunity to write a book about Delaware and its ghost stories and urban legends. Delaware is where my story begins. I was born and raised here and have had more experiences in the seventeen-plus years that I've lived in Delaware than most would want to have in a lifetime. (That could be taken as good or bad, depending on how you see it.) I'm not saying that I am anything more than anyone else, but that I have had the fortunate, or unfortunate, exposure to the paranormal from a very early age. As we travel through the great state of Delaware and explore its history, ghosts, and urban legends, I will take you on a personal journey that spans at least four generations of my family. I discovered during the writing of this book how much of an impact the paranormal/supernatural and spiritual realms have influenced my family over the years. The only way I can really describe it or put my finger on it is to say that there is "something" in my family bloodline (on my mother's side) that seems to have been passed down through the generations. Through the writing and research into my family for this book, I have really come to embrace that side of my family and see the extremely positive impact that it has directly on my immediate and extended family.

Where does one really begin to tell this tale of family, ghosts, spirits, the history of Delaware, and all those things combined? It's taken three-plus years to figure that out, and it really didn't start to all come together until the final weeks leading up to when the manuscript was due for this book.

I am extremely grateful for the opportunity to keep writing and sharing in the "global" experiences of the ghost and spiritual phenomena that has seemed to really awaken over the past few years or more. I know that I have to directly attribute the public side of the paranormal to this awakening (again, good or bad), and that without the public attention that it has drawn, none of this would really have been possible. I still remember when my now-editor, fellow writer, and friend, Dinah, first approached me and my group CCPRS (Chester County Paranormal Research Society, www.chestercountyprs.com). She was looking for help and answers as it related to the paranormal and very specifically to the geographic location of Valley Forge and Phoenixville, Pennsylvania. Thus, her book *Ghosts of Valley Forge and Phoenixville* is a must read, as it was the first book for the paranormal series that has now grown and expanded so much with Schiffer since then. It also highlights the "early days" of CCPRS as we were really starting to come together as a group and expand upon theories and techniques that I had developed independently over the years on my own. The year 2006 is when all of that took place and CCPRS would have not had its initial success or launch into the public spotlight if it had not been for the direct influence and diligence on the part of Dinah herself. She worked very hard to find the cases and investigations for the group as I can fondly remember that first investigation at the Chamber of Commerce office in Phoenixville, Pennsylvania. Oh, how far we've come since then! It was because of Dinah reaching out and letting CCPRS be involved with the research and investigating for her book that I was given the opportunity to write *Ghosts of West Chester,* and my then-wife was able to write the book *Philadelphia Haunts.* These three books all share common ground as they span and overlap in the timeline of the evolution and growth of CCPRS as an investigating team. There are stories and investigations that appear in all three books that are tied together and involve the same "players" of the group.

It was all of these experiences and the dedication of the core of the group, more specifically Carol Starr, that led to my second book, *Haunted Gettysburg,* which we co-authored together. Carol is another person whose direct influence, dedication, and passion for the field led to the completion of another important book and the continued success that CCPRS has had over the years.

My now co-author, Gerry Medvec, has directly contributed to the completion of this book. Originally, he was someone helping to gather the research, chase down leads, and perform some of the interviews for stories, as well as put the stories together. It only seemed fair and the right thing to do to expand his role to co-author. I cannot thank him enough for his contributions and dedication to this book and helping me to stay on track to complete it.

So, I hope that you will enjoy the journey that we are going to take you on as we explore the stories and experiences throughout the state of Delaware. I promise that it will be enlightening, entertaining and eye-opening for you.

Now, let us begin this journey…

~Mark Sarro

Some Delaware History

During the sixteenth century, what is now Delaware was perused often by several European kingdoms, including Spain, Portugal, and the Netherlands, but none of them found it very interesting. It was not until the early seventeenth century when someone laid claim. And, it was quite by accident. Samuel Argall, deputy to Thomas De La Warr, governor of Virginia at Jamestown, was sailing from England to Jamestown in 1610, when a storm funneled his ship into an odd bay. Here, he found protection from the sea and decided to name the waters De La Warr Bay after his leader. Purportedly, the governor never visited the waters or landfall that was named after him. It took until 1631 for the first Europeans to actually set foot on Delaware soil and construct a settlement. This was done by about thirty Dutchmen near the banks of Lewes Creek in southern Delaware. Today, this is Lewes, Delaware and the creek has been transformed into the Lewes and Rehoboth Canal. However, a year later, the colony was visited by Captain David Pietersen de Vries, head of a Dutch trading company, and co-founder of the settlement. He found all of its citizens dead and their buildings torched by the locals. The Dutch settlement, call Zwaanendael (Valley of the Swans) is remembered today by the Zwaanendael Museum in Lewes, Delaware.

Seven years later, on approximately March 29, 1638, the Swedes anchored their first colony in the region near present-day Wilmington, Delaware, under the guidance of Peter Minuit. This became the first permanent European adventure in the Delaware Valley region. The exact spot became known as "The Rocks" on the Christina River (after the Swedish Queen) and is today located at the base of Seventh Street. By far the most famous of early Swedish leaders was Governor Johan Printz, who for ten years (1643-1653), brought growth and prosperity through trade with the natives, and peace with the then-nearby Dutch settlement at Fort Casmir. The little colony clung hard to its tenuous roots into the New World soil. After Governor Printz was succeeded by Johan Rising as governor, all bets were off. He immediately waged war against the Dutch and stole Fort Casmir, which was on the site of the present-day town of New Castle.

The Swedish takeover did not last for long. In 1655, Dutchman Peter Stuyvesant sailed from New Amsterdam (what is now Manhattan, New York) commanding a Dutch naval fleet. He smashed Swedish resistance, reclaimed all Dutch ground, and captured all Swedish property, thus ending Swedish rule in Delaware. One of the legacies left to Delaware by the Swedes, along with many societal influences, is Old Swede's Church (Holy Trinity), built in 1698, still having Sunday services at 606 North Church Street in Wilmington. It is one of the oldest Protestant churches in North America. Up until the time of the Revolution, in 1776, Delaware was passed back and forth amongst many "owners." After enough football antics to fill a Super Bowl, Delaware finally declared its independence from Great Britain, and Pennsylvania, when it signed the Declaration of Independence in 1776. Later, in 1787, it was the first to ratify the United States Constitution, earning Delaware its official nickname, "the First State."

Here are some fun facts about Delaware:

- The state bird is the Blue Hen chicken. While usually ridiculed by non-Delawareans, the Blue Hen is the main contender in the bloody game of cock fighting. The militia raised by Delaware for the Revolutionary War used this bird as their mascot.
- The state bug is the Ladybug.
- The state drink is milk. Yes, we got it.
- The state fish is the Weak fish (it's not funny!).
- The state flower is the peach blossom. By 1825, Delaware was the leading producer of peaches in the country. Unfortunately, blight wiped out every orchard by the late 1800s.
- The state fossil (a fossil mascot?) is the Bbelemnitella Americana, a squid-like critter.
- The state mineral is sillimanite.
- The state tree is the American Holly, thanks to Sussex County, Delaware being the country's largest grower in the U.S. in the 1930s. The holly was sold for Holiday decorations.
- And finally…the state song (anyone can have their own song these days) is "Our Delaware" by George B. Hynson and William M.S. Brown. Hynson wrote the words; Brown wrote the music. It was published in 1906, but was so sappy, it was not adopted by the state's General Assembly until 1925.
- Today, Delaware is one of the few states without a state sales tax, making it one of the best states in the Union.

Haunts of a Generation

The Beginning: From Mark Sarro

I conducted an interview with my grandmother, Mary Bensinger, about the paranormal and spiritual experiences faced by her parents, seventeen siblings, and herself over many years. My mother's mother, Mary, is the matriarch of our family. She is the glue that has kept the family together through the decades. At the time of this writing, she is 94 years young and still a major family influence. Her love and support has illuminated my successes, and made my life wholesome. Our family's story in Delaware begins with my grandmother's parents, Elizabeth Nardo and Frank Mancari. They were Italian-born immigrants who came to America in pursuit of "the dream" and to make a new start here, specifically, in the state of Delaware. My great-grandfather came over when he was eighteen. My great-grandmother arrived when just a baby. They were both green-card-carrying Italian immigrants and remained so until their dying days.

Elizabeth married Frank when she was thirteen years old and had her first child, Mary (my grandmother), within a year. My grandmother was born on June 10, 1917. She is the oldest of eighteen children. Six of them, however, died as babies who fell to various illnesses that were prevalent at the time. Today, there are seven siblings who are still alive, including her.

My grandmother recalled where she was born and some of the events of her younger years:

> I was born in Wilmington, Delaware, at 4th and Tatnall Streets, in a little house that my parents rented. Not too long after I was born, we moved to an apartment on Front Street. The apartment was above a saloon/restaurant that my father owned and operated. He had worked as a cook at the Hotel DuPont, and, from there, went to work with DuPont as a blaster/demolitionist working with explosives. [I have his original how-to book called *DuPont's Hand Blasters Guidebook*. It is a little unassuming book full of information on how to set explosives and perform dangerous tasks.] Not too long after that, there was an explosion that took place at the factory that made him realize that he wanted out. That is when he decided to open the saloon.

My grandmother had a tough life from the time she was a toddler. She had contracted rheumatic fever, wasn't able to walk, and was bedridden for over a year. It was a long recovery, but she eventually was back in school. Then, she was forever helping around the house. Some of her earliest memories are of standing on a chair stirring a pot to help with dinner, or of changing her sibling's diapers.

> They put me in a Catholic school for a year. They wanted me to have my communion and they thought that was the only way I would get it. I really hated it.

Her Italian-Catholic mother continued to have babies. My grandmother was taking over more household responsibilities as more siblings appeared.

> When I was getting ready to go to public junior high school, my father said, "No, you're not going back to school! You are going to stay home and help your mother with the children." I was so devastated, but I had no choice and had to do what my parents told me.

Mary was only 12 at that time.

My grandmother was 19 years old when she first realized that her next door neighbor, Lawrence Bensinger, would be the one that she would marry. Mary recalls the day she first noticed him: "He was roller skating on the sidewalk and was showing off in front of me and I was impressed. I fell in love with him," she said with a cute smile and a twinkle in her eye as she remembered that day. In order to date, they would sneak off into the night to see each other away from the prying eyes of their families. Her father certainly would not approve of the courtship, so she had to take great care and keep it hidden. My grandfather's sister-in-law, his brother's wife, Kittie, had given them a car to use and told them to elope. Since my grandmother had just learned of her pregnancy, time was in short supply. Soon they would run off and elope in Elkton, Maryland. All the while, Mary's parents had no idea how serious the relationship had become. Later, my grandmother would go back to her marriage certificate, cross out "1940" and write in "1939.." She didn't want anyone to know that she was pregnant before they got married.

Larry Bensinger, (Top Left) Mary Bensinger (Top Right), Frank Bensinger (Bottom Left), Patricia Bensinger (Bottom Right). Circa 1942, before my Grandfather went off to the Pacific Campaign.

My Grandfather, Larry Bensinger, before going off to war.

Although they were now married, they continued to live a secret life apart from each other in their neighboring family homes, as they had done during their courtship. My grandmother knew it was just a matter of time before her parents would learn of the marriage and pregnancy. She had decided to approach her mother first, hoping she would be accepting, but all her mother said was, "You can't stay here. Your father will not be happy about this!" It was immediately after telling her mother of her situation that she moved next door to her husband's house with his family.

Soon they were able to purchase the first house of their own on Montgomery Street in Wilmington, Delaware.

Then Pearl Harbor happened. The United States went to war. My grandfather heard the call of duty. He enlisted in the Navy and became a "Seabee," which is the Naval Construction Force directly responsible for building and defending strategic air strips and bases that were throughout the Atlantic and Pacific campaigns. Initially, he was stationed locally, but was then transferred to Port Hueneme in California, and, from there, he was shipped off to the Aleutian Islands for nearly two years until the invasion of Okinawa, Japan. In December of 1944, an intense typhoon which would later be known as "Typhoon Cobra" ravaged the Pacific and Pacific Naval Fleet. Many ships were sunk during the storm. My grandfather often talked about that storm and the intensity and destructive force that he had to endure.

On April 1, 1945, the Marines, along with battalions from the "Seabees," stormed the beaches of Okinawa. He never liked to talk about the horrors that he viewed on the beach. He often told one of my uncles that there was "no honor" in some of the things that he witnessed. He was wounded in action there and received a purple heart. Ten years later, he would have surgery to remove shrapnel from his back that he received on Okinawa.

My grandmother was home with two children, Patricia and Frank, when my grandfather went to war. She too was called to join the war effort and went to work for the Pennsylvania Railroad, leaving her mother to care for the children. She was also wounded when a scaffold fell, hitting her on the head, causing a near-fatal fractured skull. Once she recovered, she went to work for Continental Can, a factory that made bottle caps, where she worked for over twenty-five years, until it closed.

[In her 50s, my grandmother finally decided to go back to school to get her high school diploma. She worked hard and graduated at the top of her class. It was something that she had wanted to pursue her whole life.]

Lawrence Bensinger returned home from the war and became a motorcycle police officer for the City of Wilmington Police Department. He stayed on the force for about five years and then went to work for Chrysler in an army tank manufacturing plant. Several years after being there, the plant switched over to making cars. He stayed there as a foreman until his retirement in the 1970s. He died in 1988.

My Grandfather and
his "War Buddies"
in Tanaga, Aleutian
Islands. Circa 1944.

The Tanaga
Coastline. Circa
1944 in the
Aleutian Islands.

A TASTE OF WINE ON A FINE AFTERNOON

This is the earliest family story related to the paranormal. It does not take place in Delaware, but in Italy, where my great-grandfather spent his childhood. I have included it because it is the launch point for all other spooky family tales.

It was a bright and sunny afternoon in the Italian countryside of the quiet little town of Francavilla Angitola, a small hamlet that borders the town of Filadelphia in the Province of Vibo Valentia, in the region of Calabria. Frank and his three pals strolled along through the hills and fields that surrounded the town. They were 8-10 years old, with Frank being the oldest, if not the wisest. Frank, a bit mischievous, a bit wild, but always thinking, was the unassuming leader of his "Band of Rebels." His town was small and everyone knew the kinds of trouble the boys could generate. Everyone in the sleepy village kept a watchful eye on Frank's gang. They may have been young, but were certainly capable of doing things that would make some 20 year olds blush.

On the edge of town stood a beautiful old church; it wasn't lavish or extravagant, but had the charm of ancient Europe. The church had an off white, stucco exterior with a pair of darkly stained doors that spanned nearly half of the front wall. There was a steeple that rose high above the doorway with a giant bell that would ring on every quarter hour. There were four immaculate, stained-glass windows that lined either side of the church, as well as a large one centered above the front doors, all depicting Roman Catholic effigies. The roof was black in color and did little to reflect the sun. By the way, the church was angled – it guaranteed that, as the sun set and rose, it would illuminate the interior through the windows in such a way that it *could* have been that beacon of hope, warmth, and love that all churches aspire to provide.

On this particular afternoon, Frank found the church unusually inviting. One of the front doors was left open. As an altar boy, he knew better than anyone that there were no services taking place that would require the door to be open. It was hot. He was thirsty and he knew of no better way to quench that thirst than to partake of the sacramental wine. Because of his position as altar boy, he knew the ins and outs of the church very well.

"Come on fellas!" he said jovially, as he motioned towards the church. Without question or pause his pack moved with him towards the church entrance. They trusted in "Frank, the wise," and although from time to time, they may have gotten in a bit of trouble, they usually won more than they lost.

Frank climbed the steps ahead of them and stood at the open door of the church facing inwards. "See! No problems!" he said, turning to his mates as he smiled and raised both hands to reassure them.

Despite the bright sunny day, the church seemed eerily dark, but still Frank moved inwards past the doors and into the church. One by one, the pack followed him in. They walked through the vestibule and stopped at the beginning of the center aisle that led to the altar at the far end of the building.

"Okay, this is gonna be easy. I know exactly where it is. Stay here and I'll be right back," Frank spoke reassuringly to his friends. He began to tear off down the aisle towards the altar when, out of nowhere, the once-open door of the church slammed shut with a thunderous *wham!*

The boys jumped. His friends ran to the door to try and open it, but the door would not budge.

Frank was still standing in the aisle about twenty-feet away from the others as the panic engulfed them. His friends crowded the handle and pounded the door. Frank shoved past them to get to the handle knowing that his friends must have been doing it wrong.

He turned the handle. The handle worked, but the door didn't open. It seemed frozen. The youngest of the group was stricken with terror and fear as tears began to stream down his face. After all, these boys were all younger than 10 years old, and when an ancient church door closes by itself and refuses to open, you can't expect too much from them...except for Frank.

Frank was cool, collected, and tried his best to maintain order, but he, too, started to feel the creeping sensations of panic and fear. As much as he tried to tell himself that this was okay, he felt that something far worse was about to happen. Puzzled, he stood and stared intently at the door.

The feeling of dread was now beginning to spread as a second friend started crying. Frank slowly turned around and leaned back against the door; he was facing the aisle towards the altar when he saw it. In the aisle, less than thirty-feet from where they all stood, a dark mist took form. It was floating in air three-feet above the ground. As the boys watched, the size and dimension of the black mist started to grow. Hysteria overtook all of them as they watched in dismay.

Almost in unison they turned to the door and began shrieking and hammering with both fists, screaming for help. Terror consumed them as the object behind them got closer and grew bigger. Frank turned to look again, and, this time, he saw another form start to take shape on the far aisle to the left on the other side of the pews. This form was the opposite of the dark mist. This one seemed to illuminate with an unearthly, white light as it materialized.

Due to their a mindless frenzy, and with Frank's friends screaming, crying, and pounding in such a raucous mode, someone outside finally heard them.

Meanwhile, Frank's mother's intuition sensed that something was wrong. She immediately stopped what she was doing and went outside, making her way across the town. As she walked she would stop and ask everyone, "Have you seen Francis?" And each person would respond, "Yes, he was with the boys and was heading that way!" They would all point into the same direction.

Frank's mother was diligent and slowly made her way across the town where she happened upon a woman who was hanging laundry in her side yard. "Did you happen to see my Francis come through here?" she asked with a concerned look on her face. The church was now in sight. "Yes, he went into the church with the boys!"

Frank's mother continued on to the church. As she neared the steps, she could hear the boys shrieking in terror and pounding on the door. They were begging for someone to come and let them out. In a panic herself she charged up the steps and pulled on the doors, but without success. Over the noise she tried to reassure the boys through the closed door that she was going to get some help. She turned and rushed down the stairs towards the house where the priest lived.

She made her way to the priest's door and began pounding and shouting at the door like an 8 year old. The door swung open quickly, and a disheveled old priest, just roused from a mid-afternoon nap and trying to snap on his religious collar, huffed.

"What is it you want?" he asked gruffly.

"Oh, please come quickly! The boys... The church door is stuck... Come please!" she stammered and stuttered as she motioned back towards the church. The priest, without hesitation, came out the door and went along with her at a hurried pace, making their way to the top of the steps outside the church door.

The boys were still screaming and carrying on, praying to be let out in between their cries and pounding on the door. The priest went for the door, grabbed the handle and turned it. With a peculiar rush of air the door swung open and the boys fell out through the door and into the arms of the priest. They were in hysterics and fearfully said that there were ghosts in the church!

Frank was still facing the other direction, down the aisle towards the altar. He seemed entranced by the events that had just played out before him. It wasn't until he heard his mother calling him directly that he was able to snap out of it and turn to face her. She gasped as he turned, for his skin was pale white. He stood there silent and withdrawn; he was visibly shaken by the unearthly incident that just terrorized him, almost in shock.

"Frank! What did you see? What is going on there?" his mother demanded.

"Uh, I dunno momma... I saw... I saw nothing." He answered without emotion or with any sense of urgency.

The others were now all clamoring around the priest who had brought the boys down the steps and stood in the quiet street. They were stuttering and gasping for air as they choked away their few remaining tears. They were starting to calm down.

It was clear that the boys had a paranormal experience that day while locked in the church. Something, or someone, was intent on keeping them inside, and scaring the *who-done-it* out of them. Were they trying to teach them a lesson? Were they simply playing with the boys because they knew that they could, or was it something else entirely?

Why would two spirits that seemed to be polar-opposite of each other appear in the same place within a church? In the biblical Roman Catholic sense, was this the appearance of an angel and a demon, both showing interest in the boys? Which spirit started the event? Which one closed and locked the door? Were these boys being made an example of by the light spirit as a means to "scare them straight?"

It is a tale that is not too unheard of or uncommon. I think we can speculate and draw our own conclusions.

New Castle County Background, in Short

New Castle was originally founded by the Swedes, but in its early history, ownership of the land bounced back and forth between European powers like a tennis ball at Wimbledon. The Dutch West India Company took the territory from the Swedes, naming it New Amstel (which sounds more like a beer than a town). Only a couple years later, in 1664, they turned the deed over to James, the Duke of York, who promptly kicked every Dutchman out of the area and changed the town name to New Castle. The English held their ground until 1673 when the Dutch attacked and retook the town. They renamed it (guess what?) New Amstel again. But only a year later, the whole place was given back to the English, thanks to the Treaty of Westminster on February 9, 1674 (what?). The name was changed back to New Castle (of course) and the entire region of what today is the state of Delaware was made part of the colony of New York (make up your mind!). A short time later, this same region was given to William Penn and made part of the colony of Pennsylvania (OMG!) Finally, at the time of the Declaration of Independence in 1776, Delaware not only declared itself free from the British Empire, but also from Pennsylvania.

Today, old New Castle exudes colonial warmth, enticing a tourist trade with cobblestone streets, eighteenth-century architecture and eclectic dining.

Middletown – A Centered History

In a state whose entire running length is edged by ocean, bay, and river, and with many sailable inland rivers, Middletown, Delaware was the rare colonial town not on a navigable waterway. Its life started as a tavern planted on an old road halfway between Odessa, Delaware and Bohemia Landing, Maryland—that puts the tavern/town in the middle. This road was the shortest distance between the Atlantic Ocean and the Chesapeake Bay, with ox-drawn wagons the high-speed lines of the day, dragging produce and other materials to and fro. The land warrant was originally owned by Adam Peterson in 1675. When his widow married Londonderry, Ireland native David Witherspoon, they opened Witherspoon's Tavern at the corner of King's Highway and the crossroad, the intersection known as Mrs. Blackston's Corner. This was in 1762.

In 1861, the first town council of Middletown decided that the town should be one square mile in size. Land was marked out one-half mile in all four directions, starting at Mrs. Blackston's Corner. This box design gave Middletown the nickname of "the Diamond Town of the Diamond State."

Today, Middletown has grown exponentially in population and territory, supporting massive school districts and numerous shopping malls. A fire destroyed the upper portion of Witherspoon's Tavern on February 14, 1946, but the first floor remains with its cornerstone still in place.

Marion of Middletown

Mike halted, as if by decree, and yanked his jaw off his chest. The doll shouldn't wink. While it had movable eyelids, they could not close while the doll was sitting up unless they were physically pushed down and held down. Otherwise, they simply popped open. So the doll shouldn't wink.

This American Girl doll was bought a dozen years earlier. He'd bought it because of its resemblance to Marion – similar square jaw, accurate hair color, same mid-length hair style. It was *always sitting up* on that chair and had for years. So, it shouldn't wink.

Mike walked to the chair with trepidation and picked up the doll.

"Nothing different about it," he said thoughtfully, as he turned it sideways, backwards, and upside down. *Maybe I imagined it*, he thought, then said out loud, "Marion, is that you?"

Mike and Marion Flynn met in July of 1978, and had been married about thirty years. She died of lung cancer on Christmas Day, 2008. Mike's love was deep and he always had the greatest respect for Marion. He was even envious of some of her ease with people and getting them to like her. Everyone liked Marion. She should have lived to a riper age. Her grandmother lived ninety-six years. Even with a triple heart bypass fourteen months earlier, Marion should have lived past fifty-three.

"Why did she have to go?" Mike often wondered with woe.

The official report on Mike's doll inspection: no reason for doll to wink. He set it back on its permanent spot on the chair.

Then he noticed the room swiftly fill with a presence, a chill, something ethereal but palatable, something familiar.

"Marion, it's you! I knew I didn't invent seeing that doll wink. It *was* you! Thanks, honey, for another sign." Mike was satisfied. Since her death he'd asked for and received various indications that Marion was still with him.

But the wink of an eye wasn't the first, nor the last, sign that skeptic Mike would get from the afterlife. Mike was a skeptic of a higher level. He did not believe in the physically unproven out-of-box claims of UFOlogists, spiritualists, ghost hunters, or even holy men. Fables of Loch Ness didn't float his harpoon boat.

The Flynns moved into the Airmont house in April 1996. Marion retired in 2004 from the State of Delaware. She was excited about starting her own accounting business from home. But she wasn't retired for two weeks from the State when they asked her to come back.

"I don't care where you work; that is an extremely rare situation, especially in today's cut-throat working environment," Mike commented.

That was Marion. Hard working, dependable, and a fun-loving personality kept her phone number in her boss's speed dial.

"If Marion wasn't so special, the boys and I wouldn't miss her so much. But understand; even though I miss her, I keep that separate from 'ghosts.' My loss did not invent these stories. If I didn't experience these things, there would be no stories. First of all, I can *feel* her in this house. Every day. I don't need a manifestation. Her presence is here. Maybe it's her job to be here. She hated being bored, doing nothing. She loved busyness."

After Marion's death, Mike was told by a spiritualist that sometimes a loved one's spirit returns to visit in animal form.

Early summer of '09, while working in the garage, two chimney swifts flew in and alighted on a chain that hung across the back of the open garage door. The chain was not visible if you were three or four feet away from the garage, so how the birds knew there would be a place to land on a chain just inside the doorway was just one mystery. The two birds landed, sat side by side and stared at Mike. He was no more than ten feet away at the back of his garage facing out. All parties stared at each other for about two minutes. Birds would never normally do that.

"Marion, is that you?" Mike asked his favorite question. He felt it was; at the very least, he knew it was a sign from Marion. The birds were there for a purpose. He then took a step towards them. All birds would fly off in frenzy. These birds did not. They didn't budge. They stared for another minute, *then* flew off. It was one of the most unusual moments in Mike's life. He felt sure it was Marion.

Getting signs from Marion was constantly on Mike's agenda. While he did not always receive one, the signs he did get were always convincing, usually wonderful. But one night, a sign came that made him wish there were no such things as signs.

The Doll Babies; on the right is the Doll Baby that winked from the story.

The winking Doll Baby.

Several months after the birds, while trying to fall asleep after retiring, Mike heard a pitiful wailing, a crying from an unseen female. He had not fallen asleep, so he knew it wasn't a dream. The crystal -clear cries came from somewhere either in the room or just outside. They were long, soulful cries. Many of them. It was Marion, her voice, her tone, and her distress. There was no doubt. Mike mourned at the plight-filled sounds of his late partner. After a nightmarish long time, the cries subsided and rationale stormed in to save the day.

The bedroom where the voice of his wife's ghost is heard crying out to him in agony.

Mike hopped from bed to see if it was the wind howling past the bedroom windows as often happened during storms. Curtains were yanked back and the window flung open. No wind. The eerie evening was calm as outer space.

In rehashing the story, Mike once again hears the wail, the cry, reach out from his memory, and he cries himself. Was her spirit in torment, he worried? Why was she crying? Had he done something to hurt her? Was she in pain? Trouble? Lonely?

Mike felt part of the answer was that his partner had been robbed – robbed of the additional years of pleasure she enjoyed from everyday living, and from the companionship of her admiring husband. Plus, she'd just had a brand-spanking-new grandson to enjoy and had been wishing for a second. Maybe she missed Earth.

At another time, Mike was brooding in his Florida room. He was missing Marion again. As often happened, her energy suddenly swept in like an army of Merry Maids. He quickly asked her for a sign.

"I'm always looking for that golden egg of absolute proof that Marion's spirit is here, something physical, beyond feelings alone," he said. "I got up and walked into the living room. Again, I asked her: "Marion, are you here? I think you're here. I feel you're here, *but I want to know you're here.* Can you give me a sign?"

Mike waited a prickly ten minutes for drama to unfold; a flying glass, the classic picture-falls-off-wall, or the shave-and-a-haircut thumps on the floor. Nothing.

Tired of nothingness, he glanced to the living room window and saw the mailman pull his truck up to the box at the end of his seventy-five-foot macadam driveway.

One of numerous things that used to amaze Mike about Marion was her ability to find money anywhere they went. In mall parking lots, during walks in the neighborhood, or at the beach, Marion would find coins everywhere. Mike, conversely, never saw the money. He'd walk over coins that Marion would then discover, to both their delight and amusement.

Temporarily abandoning Marion for the mail, feeling down that he hadn't gotten a sign, he strolled out his front door and started down the long driveway. At exactly halfway down the drive, sitting dead center between the length and width of the driveway was a shiny, new penny – heads up. In the fifteen years he'd lived at that address, never before had he even seen a coin on his driveway. And Mike worked outdoors on the one and a half acres almost constantly. It happened just after he'd asked Marion for a sign. He got it. It was exactly the sign that Marion knew Mike would recognize, as if it were a wave of her hand from the beyond.

The driveway where the penny
was found in the story.

Marion's strong personality in life was something that Mike truly enjoyed and missed. That strength lost little power with her step into the beyond.

On August 10, 2011, Mike was fumbling around his walk-in closet, off the bedroom – for what, he could not remember. What happened next jolted his memory away from everything earthly to Marion. While his initial idea for going in there encompassed shoes, shirts, or slacks, the last thing he was interested in seeing was the old paint-by-number painting crafted by Marion when she was 11 years old in 1966. A simple child's rendering of a house with globs of landscape set about, the art and its gray-stained frame sat in a cardboard box with just the slightest bit of the frame visible. The picture laid face down. The box was on the top shelf about seven feet up. Mike is about five-foot-ten. Suddenly, he was infused with an irrefutable need to take the picture down and look at it. It all happened quickly and smoothly as if he were a computer programmed device without a will of his own.

The last time he had looked at the painting was a dozen years previous. He never touched that picture because he didn't want it soiled with fingerprints or dust. Though Marion was its creator, he didn't feel drawn to the picture. It was, after all, only a childhood craft project. He didn't need it to remember his wife.

But in 2011 Marion had other ideas.

Mike's fingers made the long stretch to the top shelf, retrieved the painting, and swung it down with the pastel colors of the artwork face up. Marion's name was youthfully autographed with black paint in the lower right corner.

"Okay," Mike thought to himself, "I've seen this painting before. Why am I looking at this?" He scanned the painting for some reason for Marion to *physically make him* stop what he was doing and look at her little girl craftwork. He studied the little house and the thickly painted trees for clues.

Then he turned the frame over.

In the center of the heavy, brown protective paper, written in lead pencil was the date: 8/10/66 – forty-five years ago *to the day.*

"I had no idea what date was written on the back. I hadn't looked at the painting for many, many years. If I ever knew the date, I would have forgotten long ago. Seeing the date that day hit me like a rock. It was like a voice inside me saying 'get the picture, bring it down, and look at it.' I had no reason or intention to look at that picture when I went into the closet. Something or someone made me look at it. It had to be Marion. She's the one who painted it and she's the only person who could have known the date."

If Marion's previous signs escorted Mike onto the bridge between skepticism and belief, the date on the childhood painting kicked him to the far banks, and then dynamited the bridge.

This is where the picture is stored,
up on the shelf when he was
compelled to look at it further.

The picture in the story; on the back is
the hand written date: 08/10/66.

Marion didn't limit herself to contacting Mike alone. She also kept in touch with her best friend, Janet.

Janet was best friends with both Marion *and* Mike. She was an accountant who still took care of Mike's books even after Marion's passing. Mike noted that on two occasions, Janet told him (after the fact) that Marion had confided in her that their two sons were going to get into trouble. Janet probably didn't want to interfere with Mike's handling of his own brood, so she said nothing. Fortunately, the two son's troubles, potentially serious, fizzled into silliness.

Just as a woman will confide in her girlfriend about children problems, Marion had no reservation about judging Janet's fashion decisions. Janet preferred wearing track shoes. The laces on this style of shoe were usually made extra long, not something Janet needed nor liked, so she always double knotted the laces and kept them tight. According to Mike, often, while Janet was at the house working on his books, sitting at Marion's old desk, Janet would be heard saying, "Stop that, Marion."

Mike would walk over to the desk to see Janet looking down at her shoes. Every time, one shoe lace would have the double knot undone. It was always the same shoe and only that shoe. Janet told Mike she could feel this happening. Mike knew it was Marion displaying her haunting and playful caring.

What Mike now knew about the feelings and physical experiences that his late wife Marion flung into his world had changed him. He changed, at least in the area of the afterlife, from critic to Gnostic.

"There is something going on in the afterlife. I can no longer ignore that. And while I've never totally discounted it, it was questionable in my mind until my wife passed away," he said. "It's questionable no longer."

The doll in the living room probably winked.

Locust Grove Farm – Middletown

The Locust Grove house sits along a quiet little drive in Middletown. The home was the residence of the first elected governor of Delaware, Joshua Clayton. He was a physician and political leader in the times of post Revolutionary war. He had served as an officer in the Bohemia Manor Militia during the war. It was not too soon after the war that his time as a politician began. He was first elected to the Delaware House of Assembly in 1785, as the State Treasurer in 1786, and then elected by legislature to the office of Chief Executive of Delaware in 1789. He was the last politician in Delaware to hold that title under the State Constitution of 1776. In 1792, the new framework of government was put into place, and Delawareans cast their votes and elected him to the official title of Governor. He continued to serve Delaware as a United States Senator. In 1798, while in Philadelphia to speak with Dr. Benjamin Rush about the recent yellow fever outbreak, he contracted the disease and retreated back to his home at Locust Grove where he died in August of that same year.

The grounds of Locust Grove

The Locust Grove house sits back off
the road amongst the trees.

This location came onto my "Ghost Radar" by various reports concerning different types of activity reported within the house. There is one claim about a young boy who supposedly died in the house during the early 1900s. (I could not verify this historically.) The paranormal activity consists of lights and other electrical appliances turning themselves on and off, disembodied voices being heard throughout the house, and the sense of being watched or feeling another presence when you are alone. On one of my daytime excursions around Delaware, I visited the house and was able to get a good look at it from the outside. It is an interesting old house and had an integral role in Delaware's history. Is the place haunted? There have been several reports claiming that it is, but it needs further investigation.

Wilmington-Big Town History

As the county seat of New Castle County, and the largest city in Delaware, Wilmington sports all the promise of corporate power, and all the failings of urban overcrowding. At its colonial start, it was known as Willington, after the first developer, Thomas Willing. The town, along with all of colonial Delaware, was passed back and forth to various European parties for ownership, including the Swedes, Fins, Dutch, and British. Under British rule, the town name was then changed by King George II, on a whim, to Wilmington to honor Spencer Compton, the Earl of Wilmington in England.

Wilmington experienced its biggest boom with the advent of the Civil War. Being a large port on the relatively safer waters of the Delaware River (the same one Washington crossed, about sixty-five miles up-river), allowed the city to build ships and float materials with little threat of Confederate interference. Hence, the entire region burst into the manufacturing and transporting of ships, trains, uniforms, blankets, tents, shoes, and the big one—gunpowder, plus other war materials. This continued even after the war, so that by 1868, Wilmington was the largest builder of war vessels in the United States.

At the end of the 1800s, a huge park and recreation development was put in place thanks to the enormous efforts of William Bancroft, who loved the outdoors, understood the meaning of "green." The lovely Rockford and Brandywine Parks are among his creations.

The Historical Society of Delaware now owns and operates The Old Town Hall, finished in 1800, located at 500 Block Market Street.

Haunting Stories

"Not With My Spaghetti!"

My great-grandfather, Frank, in our modern times, would certainly be known as a spiritualist for some of his views, opinions, and experiences. To further deny that there is something in my mother, Joyce Bensinger's, family that has a magical/spiritual element to it at this point would seem foolish. Frank had certain customs, and one, in particular, was the water that he would drink or use for cooking.

Frank and
Liz Mancari,
my Great
Grandparents.

He had a dowsing rod that he carved himself out of a single piece of wood. The dowsing or divining rod looked like a sling shot without the sling. The wood itself was probably less than an inch in diameter and the whole rod was no longer than ten inches or more. I was fortunate that this dowsing rod was passed down to me when he died. Anyone who has known me over the years and has been to my house would have seen it sitting on my bookshelf amongst my paranormal and spiritual books, alongside my pair of copper ones.

I never fully understood the power that these rods wielded and the intensity with which my great-grandfather used them. He would routinely use these rods on a weekly basis to go out and gather the water that he would use for drinking and cooking. My mother, Joyce, recalled:

> He would take these big five-gallon jugs with him, and when he found the water source using the dowsing rod, he would fill every one of them up!

He refused to use tap water under any circumstance. This was his way; even the spaghetti was cooked in the water that he found and gathered.

These were natural springs that were hidden all over the state of Delaware, and he would use the rod to pinpoint their exact location. My mother also recalled:

> Once he located the water, he would "tap" it and the water would simply start coming up from under the ground.

He used these rods for many years; eventually, one by one, the springs that he frequented would be shut down, filled up, or blocked off so that any public access would be prohibited. In his later years, he had no choice but to drink the water that was made available to him, but I am sure that in his mind he always protested as he knew that it was not the water that he would have preferred to drink.

Dowsing Rods have become a tool used more and more by paranormal investigators all over the world. Typically, they are made of copper and are L-shaped with a sheath of copper tubing around where the user holds them so that they can move unencumbered. The idea is that you use them as an ITC device (Instrumental Trans Communication) where you ask questions aloud and the rods can answer with a *yes* or *no* based upon the instructions you place upon them. Many investigators use them to be an indicator of when paranormal activity is present at a location. In the early days of CCPRS (my paranormal group), I purchased a pair of these rods and included them in our ITC experiments and research. I have witnessed numerous times on investigations over the years how the rods are used and how they react to the environment.

Let Me Have a Drink Before I Go

On January 16, 1920, the eighteenth amendment to the United States Constitution was instituted by Congress. This amendment was the national ratification of prohibition and the start of an "Alcohol Free" era in the United States…or so congress thought! Prohibition banned the act of manufacturing, selling, and the transporting of alcoholic beverages into and out of the United States. Prohibition would stay on as a national law until December 5, 1933, when the repeal of prohibition was passed into law with the ratification of the twenty-first amendment to the United States Constitution.

The time of prohibition was when some of the colorful parts of my Italian-American history became their brightest! The increase of organized crime became prevalent from California to New Jersey and gave rise to some of the most infamous men in American history. Bring on the bootleggers! So my great-grandfather got in on the action.

During the 1920s, Frank owned a saloon, a.k.a. "speakeasy," in Wilmington, Delaware, that was located on Front Street. My grandmother recalls living above the saloon:

> This was during prohibition, you know. It was a speakeasy that sold booze when it wasn't supposed to. He would get the liquor from some people in Chester, PA who were probably affiliated with the mafia, but *he* was never directly affiliated with them. Oftentimes we would get raided and my father would press a buzzer that rang up in the apartment. When this happened we knew that we had to get rid of the booze by pouring it down the hopper. We stored the booze in the bathroom in case this happened. My father would get arrested, but because he knew people on the department and had become "friendly" with them by bribing, he never really got into any trouble.

The risks that "Blackie" Mancari (a nickname my great-grandfather carried with him) undertook while running a speakeasy were real and dangerous. The people he associated with when purchasing alcohol were thugs and murderers. My grandmother told me of an incident where the Mafia was leaning on him to become affiliated with them and he refused; he took an awful beating from their "enforcers." Frank was always on edge after that. The police also hassled him about the speakeasy, and back in those days, the only way to stay in business was to give them a cut of the money or some other friendly bribe.

The speakeasy was a good backdrop for a ghostly saga.

It was late Friday night. It had been a rough night for Blackie and his friend, Sal. There had been one too many fights at the bar, a raid, their arrest and quick release by the police. Plus, they had to walk back to the saloon from the police station. A thought formed for Blackie. "I must keep going, if for nothing else but my family!" Running a speakeasy wasn't easy.

Blackie and Sal approached the saloon from around the corner, side by side. Blackie was rubbing the back of his neck. The usual roughing up by the police was just another item on his list of things that were checked-off as "no good."

"Ya know, I'm getting way too tired for all of this, Blackie!" Sal remarked as they reached the black, Art Deco, wood doors.

"Yeah, I know, but stop complaining! You have a job, right?" Blackie replied with an undertone of anger and frustration.

"Yeah, maybe," Sal moaned. Blackie shot him a look and Sal understood.

Blackie reached into his pocket to get his keys to unlock the door. Sal turned around and leaned up against the wall next to the door, reached down into his pocket and pulled out a cigarette, lit it, inhaled, and looked up at Blackie for approval. Blackie acknowledged his friend's pain, but at the same time, dismissed the offer of a cigarette.

"I'm gonna sleep in tomorrow, Blackie! I tell ya, I have to!" Sal spoke sarcastically but with a sense of humor.

"Just don't fall out'a the bed again, okay?" Blackie replied with a smirk as he turned the key and opened the door. Sal swung back around off the wall and stood beside Blackie as they made their way through the entrance.

Upon entering the saloon, Blackie was immediately upset by the mess on the floor.

"What the hell?" he blurted.

A table was turned over, bar stools laid on their side, and broken glass was strewn across the floor like diamonds at a jewelry store on black velvet. Blackie swiftly righted the table and stools.

Sal had lazily watched his friend cleaning up. He glanced around to see if there was an easier job for him. When his eyes hit the bar, he jolted backwards.

"Hey, Blackie," he said indignantly, tapping him on the shoulder repeatedly. "Who's that behind the bar?" Sal spoke in a loud voice as he pointed to the man standing behind the bar.

"How'd you get in here?" Blackie barked as he stood, ready for anything.

The man behind the bar was an older gentleman with a haggard face, long white beard, and tattered clothes. He was average height, but pale and thin as he stood there filling his glass and gulping down its contents from the spigot that dispensed the precious beer that was the bane and bread of Blackie's existence.

Blackie suddenly locked eyes with the man. Without a word, Blackie went to the switch panel so he could get a better look at the guy he was about to pummel for breaking into his place and partaking of his profits.

With a flick of the switch, the lights turned on – and the man suddenly vanished right before their eyes. The glass that the man was holding dropped to the floor from mid-air and broke into a million pieces, adding to the mess of glass that was already there.

Blackie turned and looked at Sal without a change in expression or emotive response and said in a low stern voice, "Grab a broom and start cleaning up." The cigarette from Sal's mouth fell to his feet. His jaw hung open like a drawbridge. Sal was stunned. He reacted like a robot to Blackie's command.

"Yeah sure, okay Blackie... Yeah, right away..." Sal responded as he scampered off to find a broom and start cleaning.

Blackie turned slowly back towards the bar where the man had just been standing, looked down at the littered floor, shook his head and knelt down to continue picking up glass. He was all too familiar with the spirits of the bar and had seen plenty, and many times. He was not that surprised that the old man had stopped by for a beer.

The saloon continued well beyond the end of Prohibition. Blackie was one of the first proprietors in town to apply and receive a liquor license to run and operate his bar legally.

The House on Jefferson Street

My grandmother's experiences continued with the spirit world and the paranormal through her childhood as her family moved from one place to the next. This story is further proof of how the ethereal has played a role in our family for generations and would continue to do so.

Elizabeth was a young mother taking care of four young children in a small house on Front and Jefferson Streets in Wilmington, Delaware. Mary was the oldest of the children, but she was still a young girl at 12 years. The house was small and she had to share a bedroom with her brothers. Frank, Liz's husband, was constantly working and hustling to provide for his family. Unfortunately, this left all the responsibilities of the household completely up to Liz.

But she had someone to help her.

Ms. Jennie was a mild mannered, quiet woman who came to help with the laundry and the other household chores. This was a time not too long after the great depression and things were still a struggle for everyone everywhere. Liz was happy to have the help and Ms. Jennie fit the role perfectly. Ms. Jennie kept her opinions to herself most of the time, but when it came to matters of the spirit realm she couldn't help but let her voice be heard. She had witnessed with her own eyes and heard with her ears odd occurrences in the home. Liz, too, was having experiences in the house that seemed unsettling. It wouldn't be until years later that she would share the most profound experience that she had in the house with her family.

Late one morning Elizabeth and Ms. Jennie sat at the kitchen table for a moment of relaxation. Ms. Jennie had gotten to the point where the laundry was half done and Liz had the children fed and dressed. Now, the kitchen was in the process of being cleaned. Liz was quietly sipping at a cup of coffee.

"Ms. Lizzie," Ms. Jennie said, "I must tell you that something ain't right about this house!"

Liz finished her sip of coffee and put the cup down on the table. She looked at Ms. Jennie with an expression of exhaustion, but without emotion. She knew instinctively what Ms. Jennie meant.

"I know, but there isn't anything that I can do about it," Liz replied in a tone that would almost signal a sign of defeat.

"There is plenty you can do! Move out of here!" Ms. Jennie exclaimed.

"Oh no. That is just not possible. How could you think that we could just up and move out of here?" Liz responded defensively.

"I don't mean any offense Ms. Lizzie; I'm just saying that there is something wrong with this house!"

Ms. Jennie spoke with a passion and conviction that demonstrated great concern for Liz and her family.

"Well, maybe you need to explain what exactly you mean?" said Liz in a more inquisitive, yet still defensive tone.

"Ms. Lizzie, you've got ghosts in this house!" Ms. Jennie exclaimed with excitement.

Liz paused for a moment as she took another sip from her cup, but said nothing. "Ms. Lizzie, I know you have not been well, with you losing a baby last year and now another one is sick, too. I feel there is something evil going on here!"

Liz accepted Ms. Jennie's words. They hit her in a way that she could not deny. Finally, it was out in the open. She had been physically and emotionally at her tipping point with all that had happened over the past year or so. Having lost several children within months after they were born had taken a toll in ways beyond normal communication. Now, with another one of her children sick to the point that there was little hope of the baby's survival, she was starting to lose hope in herself as well.

Liz sat back in the chair, took a deep slow breath as she looked down at the cup in her hands, and then looked at Ms. Jennie. "There have been some things that happened in the last few months that I must tell you about. Mary was awoken in the middle of the night by a hard slap across her face. She jumped up screaming and crying and ran into our bedroom to tell us what had happened. Frank awoke and immediately rose from the bed in anger. He automatically assumed that our son, Carmen, had been the one that slapped her as if it were a joke of some kind, but when he pushed the door open to scold Carmen, he was still fast asleep. Of course he woke him and yelled at him anyway, but it's clear that it was not Carmen or any one of the other children that had slapped Mary."

Ms. Jennie looked at Liz with an expression of deep concern and shock. She had no idea that the things going on in the house had evolved into personal attacks on the children.

"The baby has been crying and carrying on at all hours of the day and night and we can't seem to understand why," Liz continued. "The baby is sick, we know that, but still the baby cries and cries and I just don't know what to do anymore!" Liz explained with an increasing stress in her voice. She was visibly getting upset. Ms. Jennie stood up and went over to Liz and put her arm around her.

"I know, I know. It's gonna be alright," Ms. Jennie said. "You're a strong lady and I know all will be well."

Liz turned away from Ms. Jennie and grabbed the handkerchief out of her pocket and began to wipe her face and blow her nose.

"There is something else..." Liz paused and seemed to be hesitant to say anymore. "I found something, but I haven't the nerve to touch it or do anything with it," Liz said quietly as though she was concerned that someone other than Ms. Jennie was listening.

"What did you find?" Ms. Jennie asked.

Without saying a word, Liz slowly pointed to the middle of the kitchen floor. The floor was hardwood like the rest of the house, but one board was sticking up just enough that you could see that it was out of place.

"The floor? What's wrong with the floor?" Ms. Jennie asked with a sense of confusion.

"It's not the floor. It's what's *in* the floor," Liz stated in a soft quiet voice.

Liz stood up, strode to the kitchen counter, and grabbed a butter knife from a drawer. She turned around slowly and made her way to the floor where the loose board was, as if she didn't like the idea. She lowered to her knees and slowly, meticulously worked at the loose board with the knife. She pried up the board. Ms. Jennie looked on with bewilderment as she still didn't understand why Liz was prying up floor boards.

Ms. Jennie could sense a change in Liz. The air in the room grew heavy and emotions started to fray. Ms. Jennie walked to Liz and sat on the floor next to her. She saw fear creep across Liz's face. Liz locked eyes with her and motioned toward the open space in the floor.

In the hole of the floor lay something peculiar; there, folded neatly with a small book next to it, was a pile of clothing. Both of the items appeared to have been damaged in a fire, with burnt edges and covered with soot.

Liz and Ms. Jennie blinked at each other.

"Oh, Ms. Lizzie, that's a bad omen! You don't want to have nothing to do with that!" Ms. Jennie exclaimed.

"I am not sure what to do with them! I haven't had the nerve to touch them yet," Liz replied.

"Oh no! You don't want to touch 'em or do anything *to* them! Put the floor board back and never look at it again, if you ask me." Ms. Jennie spoke with fear and foreboding in her voice.

"I have to look at them. They are there for a reason, but I don't have the nerve. No one else knows about this except for you and me; and now that you are here, I think I must touch them and see what exactly they are!" Liz said. She leaned forward on her knees, reached down inside the floor, and slowly began to pick up the clothing with both hands.

Ms. Jennie leaned away from the hole, half expecting a volcano of evil to erupt.

Liz slowly and carefully lifted the clothes out and put them on the floor next to the open hole. Instantly, the atmosphere in the kitchen went black. A horrible sense of dread washed over both Liz and Ms. Jennie. The fear that suddenly gripped both of them sparking outward like a metal plate in a microwave.

Then, without pause, a deep, loud, grumbling voice spoke out to them from the middle of the room.

"PUT THEM BACK!"

Both Liz and Ms. Jennie looked up in fright as if the voice came from right in front of them! Yet there was no one there to be seen.

Ms. Jennie jumped to her feet and could hardly contain her terror. Liz hastily picked up the clothing and returned them neatly to their spot in the hole. She grabbed the loose floor board, smacked it in place with a driving, closed fist. She hit with such force that the board set even with the rest of the floor as though it had never been loose.

Liz rose to her feet and went to grab Ms. Jennie and sit her in her chair. But Ms. Jennie was so visibly shaken that she bounced up and paced nervously about the room.

In the next room, the baby started to cry. Liz knew that despite what had just happened, her needed moment of rest had ended. It was time to get back to caring for the baby.

Ms. Jennie excused herself from the house and left for home. My great-grandmother Liz would not share this story until many years later, long after they had moved out of that house. My grandmother noted that Ms. Jennie stopped working for her mother, Liz, after that day. The incident with the clothing in the floor was probably the final straw for Ms. Jennie, as that experience would only confirm what she had come to witness and see with her own two eyes on previous frightening occasions.

The House on Fifth Street

Great-Grandmom Bensinger, Grandfather Lawrence's mother, would experience things on the third floor walk by her and brush against her legs at the house on Fifth Street. Grandmother Mary always had a sense of uneasiness in that house. Pat, her oldest daughter, had a bedroom on the third floor. That bedroom is where a man hung himself. Great-Grandmom Bensinger would have other experiences and see the ghost of the man walking the halls and lingering in the rooms.

The Case of Mrs. Gotham

A ghost looking for her grandchild is a motivated ghost.

The houses on Turnstone Drive, in the Brookmeade section of Wilmington, Delaware, are two-story colonials, designed for families in late 1950s. One particular house, instead of the usual two-car garage and a family room, had an in-law suite built for the owner's mother-in-law. The wife was pregnant, and her mother was due to move in and help her with all child rearing necessities while the daughter went back to work.

Mrs. Gotham must have looked forward to the pleasures of granny-hood. She would get to hold the newborn, coddle, feed, even diaper change, then later teach the toddler to talk, walk, run, and learn. Like most people, she would delight in showering her grandchild with love and affection, and would sparkle from the love returned through wide innocent looks and cute coos.

But Mrs. Gotham never made it to the in-law suite that was built expressly for her. She died just weeks prior to the move, never to meet her grandchild in this life, never to pinch a cheek or give a stroller ride, never to beam at a graduation. And she had been so looking forward to it all.

Mrs. Gotham's saddened family then fell on harder times. The house had to be abandoned and it sat vacant for over a year.

It was then purchased by Les and Martha Duval, who moved in with their two children in February 1972. A large part of the charm of the house for the Duvals was the custom-made in-law suite. It had a separate side entrance, a kitchenette, full bath, and two bedrooms. They used the suite as a family room and a great play area for their two children.

Immediately after they moved in, they started to notice some oddities about the house. Doors started to open and close on their own; after someone left a room, then returned, they'd find the doors ajar. Electric and battery-powered clocks would stop at various times throughout the

Turnstone Drive in the Brookmeade section of Wilmington where the spirit of Mrs. Gotham once lived.

day. The couple would have to physically rotate the hands to the correct time to get the clocks running again. Martha would often set the washing machine to work, but it would suddenly turn itself off in mid cycle. Once, while having company, the guests both noted they heard a baby crying. Neither Les nor Martha heard the cries, but the guests were adamant. The pipes in the basement often rattled. But on a particular night that Martha would never forget, at ten o'clock, the pipes banged with such ferocity that Martha was sure the house would come down around her and the children. It was the only time Martha felt disquiet in the house.

At all times, Les and Martha could feel a presence in the home. They constantly felt watched. Many times while sitting in a room, they felt a sensation of cold air rush by them. There were no doors open, no windows open. Yet the coldness passed by like a dead woman walking.

Both Les and Martha experienced all these issues separately, but during the first couple months in the house they never discussed it. Who wanted to bring up the topic of having a ghost in the house and risk disbelief or ridicule from their partner? Each would rather think something like, "Oh, it's winter time. It must be the wind or something." The good report was that they didn't feel threatened or upset by the goings on. It just seemed so strange.

Finally, after two months of perplexing activity, Martha and Les sat in their kitchen and began sharing stories about the weird incidents they had experienced separately. Their mutual validation was a powerful release, like Niagara Falls bursting from each of them, draining stress, washing it down Turnstone Drive.

About this same time, the babysitter they had been using decided to speak up and confirm that the spirit acts were enjoyed unanimously. The babysitter also discovered that doors to rooms, closets, and cabinets opened or closed on their own after she left a room, knowing truly that she'd left the doors in the correct position. The babysitter, too, experienced the clocks stop and the pipes clang.

While all these things multiplied made the Duval's stay in their new home a bit zany, at no time did they ever feel threatened, or that their children were in danger. They liked their new home, were resolute about staying, and believed they could manage the haunting on their own.

That was until Mrs. Gotham made her entrance.

One evening, Les was about to climb the entrance hall staircase when the air around him suddenly lost heat. He paused at the bottom of the steps, looked up, and saw, to his astonishment, a short, older woman with white hair, dressed in a blue, sleeveless summer dress. She was there for only seconds, and then vanished like a Hollywood special effect.

Les raced to get Martha.

"Martha, I just saw an old woman standing at the top of the stairs. She had white hair. She looked solid – and, and then she disappeared!" He was excited and bewildered.

Martha froze in place.

"That does it! We're getting this house blessed!" she said. Martha was not about to let a ghost, no matter how old, harmless or fleeting, be an intrusive factor in her family's new home.

Martha called their parish priest on the spot. It wasn't an easy call. Her heart was in her throat over a concern that the priest might deride or chastise her for even thinking about believing in ghosts. It might be unChristian-like. The Catholic Church in the 1970s was in fact much stricter about enforcing their laws and edicts on such issues. The monsignor, however, after quietly listening over the phone to Martha's shakily told story, asked a reassuring question.

"Has any of the furniture moved around yet?" The reverend had experience with hauntings. Martha assured him nothing had moved and urged him to come quickly.

The next afternoon, Sunday, the monsignor arrived solemnly at the front door, and after a brief greeting to Martha and Les, began instantly reciting Catholic prayers for a cleansing and flinging holy water at every room, closet, hallway, and staircase. When finished, he told the family to let him know if negative issues persisted, said he'd hope to see them in church again next Sunday, and was gone.

From that instant on, the house went quiet. No Mrs. Gotham.

Later that summer of '72, while talking to the next-door neighbor couple over the side fence, Les began revealing the story of the spooky hauntings in his house and their resolution. When Les described the ghost and her clothing, the neighbors recognized the description.

"Oh, that must have been Mrs. Gotham. She was the mother-in-law who was supposed to take care of the baby. But she died before she had a chance to move in. We used to chat with her sometimes when she came to visit her daughter," the neighbor noted.

That validation gave the Duvals a little more insight into the reason for their haunting, and a bit more closure with all the feelings involved. The Duvals remained in the house a few years, then did what most people did in the '80s: They traded up.

Had Mrs. Gotham traded up? Was she at peace? Did she realize it was time wasted to remain on earth, and decide that starting her next ethereal assignment was in the best interest of all? Or did she simply go to the next house in search of her descendants?

Above Par

The man in the gray suit was not the first problem Vern had at the golf course.

Despite a lovely Wilmington, Delaware fall day that was usually available only on a postcard, Vern's mental state was a distracted zone. That Monday, October 10, 2011, was less a fun day off from work, and more of a mission to blow up Bagdad. His golf game, through the first sixteen holes, had sent his golf ball on vicious slices to the right and hellish hooks to the left. The ball suffered explosions out of sand traps and a near plunge into an under-pond grave. As a result of this poor play, Vern's nerves felt as if they were massaged by sandpaper.

Vern had looked forward to a good day of golf by himself at Porky Oliver's Golf Club in Wilmington. Over the last several years, he had toiled at a local Mazda dealer, trying to keep control of his income. The recession still encompassed the planet like a black cloud, and selling big-ticket items like cars had to leave Vern a bit foggy. Certainly, he cherished his days off, and some good golf play would normally bring relief from the stress of a life overworked. At last it finally started to do so at the 17th hole – thanks to the man in the gray suit.

The approach to the green on the 16th hole gives a good view of Green Hill Presbyterian Church with its attached cemetery. The church property (over 150 years old) and golf club property (over 100 years old) touch at the corner where the 16th green ends, and they continue together southeast to the end of the 17th hole. You must turn right off the 16th hole to the 17th tee, which lies along the edge of the cemetery. The 17th is downhill, a 179-yard par three from the blue markers.

Vern's luck changed about 1:30 p.m. He finished the 16th hole and trudged to the next with fading enthusiasm. A mid-iron club was grabbed from his golf bag and he teed up his ball. Facing the pin, the graveyard starts about twelve-feet to the left of the tee area.

Vern was ready to start his swing routine when he suddenly felt like he was being watched. He looked up and saw an elderly gentleman with white hair and long, white beard, in a gray suit and a stiff, white, religious collar, standing by the nearest graves, watching him. The fellow carried himself like a pastor.

"How's it going, son?" The old man had a polite, caring way about him.

"Not so good, Father," Vern replied with forced lightheartedness and a fake smile. He didn't feel like talking. The course had been mean to him.

"Well, at least you're playing. Hit a good one."

Vern grinned and nodded. He didn't want to encourage a long conversation since he was there to play. He put his eyes back on the ball. He pulled back his iron over the top of his head, and then swung down on the ball with a smooth, solid stroke. The ball missiled to the flag stick, hit it with a "clack" and dropped a few inches from the hole – almost a hole-in-one. It was a phenomenal shot, the kind of shot that sent Sunday golf crowds at professional events around the world into ear-shattering cheers and ballyhoo. And no matter whom the crowd was rooting for prior, the person who made that kind of a shot became their instant hero.

Vern was radiant. He'd been trying to do that all day. The moment the ball hit the pin, only seconds after the old man had said to "Hit a good one," Vern turned to the old boy to thank him for his blessing. There was no one to thank. The gray suit was gone. Where did he go?

Vern looked around. He wasn't behind the nearby tombstones, they were too small; not amongst the cars in the church parking lot either. The man was too old to play hide-n-seek. He wasn't behind the bushes back near the 16th green; Vern could see through the branches. There was a funeral service in progress for the late Mrs. Elaine Clarke farther back in the cemetery. But to cover the distance between the edge of the cemetery and the funeral tent in a few seconds, Vern rationalized, the octogenarian either burst into an Olympian sprint, or vanished through a Houdini trap door in the ground.

Vern asked other golfers that he saw if they'd seen the old gentleman. But no one recalled seeing anyone of that stand-out description. Eventually, one of the golfers, perhaps tired of Vern's insistence that the old gentleman *must be around somewhere*, blurted out, "Well then you must have seen a ghost!"

Vern didn't believe in seeing dead people, and wanted nothing to do with that subject, period. He had always been a granite-based skeptic pertaining to ghosts.

He still doesn't believe in ghosts. He just believes in the old gentleman in the gray suit, and the miraculous birdie on a par three.

Delaware City – A Past in its Future

Delaware City is known for two of its tourist features: the historical Chesapeake and Delaware Canal, and Fort Delaware. Originally called Newbold's Landing, after the Newbold family of New Jersey who purchased the land, Delaware City, almost from its outset, had building plans in 1826 to rival Philadelphia, Pennsylvania (just thirty-five miles upriver) as the leading river port and commerce center on the east coast. This never happened. What did happen was that a waterway through the Delmarva Peninsula, to shorten the trade route from Philadelphia to Baltimore, Maryland was planned. In 1802, the Chesapeake and Delaware Canal Company was formed and the digging began two years later between Delaware City and Chesapeake City. The Canal opened in 1804 at 13 $^5/_8$ miles in length.

Sitting one mile off the banks of Delaware City, on Pea Patch Island in the middle of Delaware River, is one of the east coast's most haunted, and best preserved antique fortresses, Fort Delaware. Built after the War of 1812, it was designed to protect the cities of Wilmington, Delaware, Philadelphia, and Camden, New Jersey against any invaders. It later became a massive prisoner of war camp for captured Confederates.

Today, Delaware City has the largest Historic District in Delaware with over 250 structures.

FORT DELAWARE

Fort Delaware sits on Pea Patch Island, about one mile from the shores of Delaware City. This fort was tapped to be the replacement for Fort Mifflin (the Revolutionary War-era fort that single-handedly saved Washington and his men from a crippling blow by the British). The fort went through several incarnations (a fire took out the original one) until it became the famous pentagon-shaped fort that is there today. The fort is well known for its time during the Civil War, as it was one of the largest prison camps during the war. There were so many prisoners that it had a population ten times larger than Delaware City.

The paranormal history of the fort is diverse. There have been numerous reports of full-body apparitions, disembodied voices, and physical interactions with spirits. I'm using this story as a backdrop to some of the methodology, theories, and techniques employed by the paranormal investigator.

The first time that I visited Fort Delaware was on a family excursion. I had

Outside the Fort, to the right of the Sally Port.

wanted to go there ever since my family moved to Delaware City. I had read about some of the paranormal accounts that had taken place and was eager to see and experience the fort for myself.

Timing is Everything

In a place like this, it shouldn't matter what time, day or night, you visit in order to have a paranormal experience. This will be a good opportunity to explain the reasoning and rationale behind some of the motives and procedures used during a formal investigation.

An unfortunate byproduct of television shows and movies on the paranormal is that there is a misconception that the paranormal only happens at night. This is totally and completely FALSE! You do not need to be sitting in the dark with a million watts of IR light wreaking havoc in every nook and cranny of the environment. One of the basic principals I have taught to student investigators is that you must first build a picture of the environment and the reports of activity. Usually, I will ask a client to keep a journal. This can be a tedious task, and often the client does not do it. It serves as an invaluable tool. A journal allows us to see a "snap shot" of what is occurring. It also helps to establish if there are any patterns to the type of activity being reported.

Outside the Fort, to the Left of
the Sally Port, above and next
to the flag is where the canon
demonstration takes place.

On the wall above the casemates, overlooking the
moat out towards the water.

A simple question that I pose: If the peak of the activity is happening on a Sunday afternoon at around 2 p.m., then why would you investigate on a Saturday night at 10 p.m.? It's not going to stop investigators or teams from doing the latter, but it is definitely going to impact the potential experience and possibility of gathering any physical evidence. In the same vein; would you go fishing off a pier at low tide when you know damn well that the fish will be there at high tide? Again, you wouldn't, yet this is the trap that a lot of investigators and teams fall into.

Another pitfall of working with an investigative team: You now have to factor in all of the schedules and personal lives of those involved, but ultimately it really comes down to the availability of the client. If the client is only available for you to come over on a Friday night at 8 p.m., but the activity is happening on a Sunday at 2 p.m., you go when the client is available. Although, once you begin gathering the information and "painting" that picture of what is happening, an argument can be made to the client as to why you should be investigating at one time over another. If they want answers, then they will be willing to do whatever it takes to get to the bottom of what's going in their particular situation.

In a place like Fort Delaware there are so many reports and accounts of the paranormal that there are whole books dedicated to just this one location! So, my inclinations to visit this place and perform basic tests during the "tourist" hours are justified. The same can be said of any of the following places in the tri-state area: Fort Mifflin, Eastern State Penitentiary, and Gettysburg, among many others. You do not need to lock yourself off in any of these places and spend exorbitant amounts of money to have them to yourself.

At the fort, I had decided to bring my portable ITC device with me and conduct some simple EVP and ITC environmental sessions, along with my digital camera. [See Glossary for ITC explanation] It was all I needed to conduct a preliminary investigation of the place. Besides, I always recommend that before you ever do a nighttime investigation, you should visit it in the daytime during normal operating hours. There are so many subtle nuances of a location that can be lost when you are visiting after dark. My team must have visited Fort Mifflin, Eastern State Penn, and Gettysburg a dozen times before we ever did any type of formal "after hours" investigation at any of these locations. This is part of the process that we follow and it has always proven to be a successful model for operation.

Outside the Sally Port,
the main entrance.

On the bridge to the Sally Port,
overlooking the moat.

I stepped through the main sally port and into the courtyard of the fort. The buildings and walls of the place encompass you. I stood there for a moment, basking in the sunlight and taking in my environment. I wanted to take in as much of the fort as I could, but at the same time, I did not want to be influenced by the immediate history. I hoped that by "wandering" the fort without any filters that I would have strong first impressions. If I was meant to have a spiritual event, then it would happen on its own accord and not be me forcing anything to act "on-demand."

Inside the courtyard, looking towards the back of the fort where the water lies just beyond that wall.

Instrumental Transdimensional Communication

I turned on the ITC device, put on my headphones, and began to let the device work on its own. I was monitoring the device while walking around the fort to see everything for the first time. Again, I was not going to force any communication with the spirits, and figured that if anyone wanted to communicate with me, that they would come forward on their own. The device scanned the frequencies and ticked with each passing one. The interesting thing with this piece of equipment is the amount of "chatter" that can be

Inside the "tunnels," ramparts, and casemates of the Fort; you can walk from one side all the way down the back wall and around to the right on the first and second floors inside the Fort.

The canon replicas inside the Fort. When the Fort was at full strength, it boasted over 150 guns, and strategically placed canons inside and above, along the walls. There used to be canons pointing inward towards the prison barracks; in the case of a riot, they would open fire on all who lay below.

produced in the more active paranormal locations. "Chatter" would be, for example, when an assembly of people gather and talk amongst themselves before the keynote speaker begins to talk. This is much the same in the spirit world: The device attracts them to the podium and they all talk until one steps forward and grabs the mic. I have had this experience several times. In the more active paranormal locations, the "chatter" will begin as soon as you turn on the device. The skeptic might dismiss this phenomenon as background interference coming through from the different radio frequencies. I would have to counter by saying that there is a distinct difference between the background voices of the different radio frequencies and the "chattering" voices that come through on the ITC device.

I find an older model device, well known for the "ticking" sound it produces when it changes frequencies, is actually beneficial as providing a point of reference for the other voices that are coming through. Each tick represents a frequency change on the device. When the typical radio frequency chatter is produced, you will hear the voices getting cut off, or changing dramatically from one to the next, because the device is moving through the different frequencies. Whereas, the paranormal "chatter" is a continual stream of voices that do not change as the frequencies change. It provides stronger evidence that what we are receiving is more than random radio frequencies, but actual communication from someone from beyond. Exactly where they are coming from, I don't know. This is what keeps the field of paranormal research interesting, as well as one of the inherent challenges of doing this type of work. Because there are no absolutes, we are often left to make a best guess as to what is occurring and why. This can, of course, prove to be disasterous if a poor conclusion is drawn without as much available information being provided to influence that decision, but it's a part of the journey that one must take while being a researcher.

The "chatter" that was now coming through on the device as I moved throughout the fort was an indication that there was paranormal energy present. Through the course of my visit there that afternoon, I did ask some basic and traditional EVP questions, but did not receive any direct answers. The "chatter" remained a constant, but it was becoming apparent that no one was willing to come forward and communicate. Since that time I have visited the fort several times.

The volunteers and staff at the fort do such a great job of bringing back the heyday of the Civil War. You can do a walking tour or wander about on your own and discover the fort at your own pace and on your own terms. But either way, when you encounter a re-enactor, they will transport you to that place and time and will only interact with you using the vernacular and knowledge possessed at that time. I would recommend visiting the fort to anyone who has an interest in our rich American history as well as the paranormal. It will not disappoint you in either category.

For more information you can visit the Fort's website at:
www.destateparks.com

POLK HENRY HOUSE

When I was initially doing research for this book and trying to track down locations for possible investigations, I came across a report about a building in Delaware City called the Planchette Playhouse. The reported claims (on the Internet) were that of paintings and photographs that animate, mirrors that bleed, folks being pushed down steps, a face being seen through windows from outside, etc. A plethora of paranormal treats that I felt was too good to pass up... and usually too good to be real. I was not able to track down the property; however, I did find a big, dark federal-style building that was vacant.

I decided to go into the local realtors' office to inquire if anyone knew about the building. I spoke to the receptionist; she was very pleasant. She tried to give me what information she could, but deferred me to the realtor, who was not in. Within a few hours, though, I received a phone call from the realtor and he was more than happy to give me information about the building and the name and phone number of the owner.

My next step was to call the property owner and talk to him directly about the building and possibly the paranormal activity that has been reported there. He answered the phone and we spoke briefly about my intentions. He informed me that yes, there was some activity there and that his sister-in-law had done extensive research on the history of the house as well as conducted several of her own paranormal investigations.

I was very excited to hear this news and immediately began to explore the possibilities of Gerry and me getting into the building for our own investigation. The owner was very receptive to the idea, but I knew with the book deadline only a few weeks away there would be no way that I could conduct a full investigation, review the evidence, and then write about it with enough detail that I could tell the story properly. During my discussion with the owner, it was revealed that the property was known as the Polk Henry House and that he was not familiar with it being known as the Planchette Play House.

Outside the front doors of the Polk Henry house at 3ʳᵈ and Washington Streets in Delaware City.

A week had gone by and I decided to give him another phone call to see what the next step would be. We spoke again briefly. He was more than willing to show me the property and let me come through it to take some preliminary photographs inside and outside of the building. We set a day and time the following week for us to meet him for our tour of the property.

The day came for us to meet. Gerry and I walked over to the property as I was now officially a resident of Delaware City, living only a few blocks from the house. It's a three-story building with lots of space and many rooms. Initially, the building was a private residence and then at some point became a boarding house.

When the owner arrived, we exchanged greetings and he immediately began to show us the property. He took us through the house, room by room and floor by floor, showing us the improvements he made. After the initial go round, he was happy to leave us on our own to explore and take pictures.

I really wasn't expecting to do any more than a walkthrough, but now, with this opportunity to explore on our own, I felt obliged to at least attempt a simple EVP session on the second floor where the most paranormal activity had been reported. According to the owner, the types of activity in the house was more along the lines of a classic or residual haunting and nothing like the near Hollywood reports that I had found in my initial research.

Outside to the left of the
Polk Henry House.

Carefully, Gerry and I made our way around the house as I snapped pictures. When we got to the second floor, I decided to stop and do an EVP session. This area had reports of apparitions, unusual sounds, and footsteps. It was a bright and sunny day, so it was well lit, even without electric lighting and with all of the windows covered. Initially, Gerry and I started out together in the same room. I asked a few questions aloud while recording video with my camera. After several minutes, I switched the camera back to still photographs and began snapping away. Gerry decided to go off and explore a little on his own on the other side of the second floor. I was standing in the room where the activity was reported, facing an open doorway that led to a hallway past the back stairwell, towards the backside of the house. I remained quiet, settling into the environment to see what, if anything, would happen. Standing totally still, not shifting or moving in the slightest, I snapped a few more pictures.

Suddenly it was there.

Energy. I'm not quite sure how else to describe it. It was perfectly clear, but created a visual distortion of whatever lay beyond it. I observed it as it came into the room from the doorway that led out to the hallway. It was small, not larger than a softball, although it was hard to judge since it didn't cover a large surface area (certainly not like what I saw on the shore of Cape Henlopen during our Halloween night investigation). But, it was enough that I saw it directly in front of me. I called out to Gerry and explained what I had just seen. He came

On the second floor in this room is where the energy was seen moving towards Mark. It happened in the foreground of this picture, just inside the door and to the left.

back into the room, but it was gone. We stood there for a few more minutes in the hopes that something else would happen. Unfortunately, we couldn't stay. I did not have the luxury of time as I had another appointment.

All in all, we were only in the house for about twenty to thirty minutes at most, but I was amazed by what I saw in such a brief time. I'm excited by the promise of what we could experience if we spent time there some evening when reported activity is surging.

Although I was not able to visit the location and do an investigation in time to have it for this book, I do plan on following up with the owner and his sister-in-law, who have investigated the house, to gather more information about the property. Once we have thoroughly investigated the Polk Henry House, and reviewed our evidence, there will be a case report available on: www.chestercountyprs.com. Hopefully, by the time this book is in print, the investigation of the Polk House will be completed.

I believe that there is something going on in that house, because in the short period of time I was there, I did actually see and witness something with my own two eyes.

Kent County – History, Even Shorter

It was official on June 21, 1680: New Castle County was too large, and the people in the southern regions wanted more autonomy. They formed a new county named St. Jones. Today, this is known as Kent County.

The English initially settled the region, and governing responsibilities were given to William Penn. He ordered a courthouse built for the middle county of Kent in 1697. Plans for the city of Dover were drawn up in 1717 and the city's central location made it proper to be titled the capital of Delaware, which it still is today.

Aside from Dover's political importance and being the home of the massive Dover Air Force Base, Kent County has the distinction of being home to manufacturer ILC Dover, located in Frederica, Delaware. They are the makers of spacesuits for the Apollo and space shuttle astronauts. The model "A7L" suite was worn by Neil Armstrong and Buzz Aldrin on the Apollo 11 mission, when both men walked on the moon.

Dover – Capital History

The state capital of Dover is the fastest growing city in Delaware thanks to a growing need for government jobs, commercial investments, and the massive Dover Air Force Base. Dover AFB has the difficult honor of housing the Air Force Mortuary Affairs Operations, the largest mortuary in the Defense Department. It is their gruesome task to process the bodies of military people who die in the line of duty, no matter which branch they serve. These facilities have also been used to assist in extreme civilian cases, like the Challenger Shuttle disaster, the Jonestown mass murder/suicides, and Space Shuttle Columbia explosion.

Dover is also home to the Dover International Speedway, where the FedEx 400 and the AAA 400 are held annually, as well as numerous other NASCAR sponsored events. The 135,000-seat stadium makes Dover the largest race stadium in the mid-Atlantic area. It encircles the "Monster Mile," considered one of the tougher concrete tracks.

Dover Downs Hotel and Casino (former owner of the Speedway) also contributes to tourism and money making, although perhaps more for the casino and less for the gamblers. The 500-room AAA-rated Four Diamond Hotel is one of the largest in the state. The casino houses 2,500 slot machines and sixty poker tables with a variety of games. It sports nine fine restaurants that serve everything from a deli sandwich to a four-star experience, with plenty of alcohol to wash it all down. The stress from seeing that ghost on The Green in the center of town can be rinsed away with aromatic oils and certified hands at the hotel's spa.

MARK'S STORY: THE EARLY YEARS

In 1979, my family was just starting out. I was 5 years old, my older brother was 13, and my sister was 12. That year was difficult for my family. My father's construction company filed for bankruptcy, and with it, we lost the house. My parents were eager for a fresh start, so it was decided we move downstate to Dover, the capital of Delaware. My parents had found a nice little stone house on Main Street in the heart of town. It was just the right size so that my siblings and I had our own rooms. My mother, Joyce Bensinger, recounts the beginning of our time in Dover:

Times were hard. The market dried up for home builders as many, including us, faced bankruptcy. Since jobs were scarce in the Wilmington area, my husband, Nick, had to follow the work. So we moved to Dover.

I had mixed feelings about the move. We left a lot behind; a home, our family, and friends, but Dover represented a new start.

I didn't know much about Dover, only the memory of driving through town years before with my parents on the way to the South Bowers Beach. I had always admired the grand houses along State Street, pointing out my favorites as we passed. Now I was excited. We were actually going to live on State Street, although in a more modest rental home near the hospital. The family who owned this early 1900s home was living in another state. Like our family, employment took them elsewhere.

The house that Mark lived in for a year with his family; this is where his paranormal story begins.

Moving day came. The three kids, Mark (5), Sherri (12), and Nicky (13), were happy about their new bedrooms. Extra boxes, like Christmas decorations, were put in the basement.

This basement was a concrete marvel with extra-wide, waist-high concrete shelves jutting far into the room; perfect for keeping our boxed treasures off of a potentially wet floor. I never saw such a unique shelf system running along the length of the house. In any case I am not a basement person – they give me the creeps.

Once we moved in, I had a wonderful sense of "homecoming," like a warm embrace of a family member. This powerful sense of belonging was out of the ordinary. In any move I made in the past, a house felt empty until we had settled in and made it a home. This house immediately felt like home.

Over the course of those first few weeks in the house, the neighbors would stop by and issue a warning to my parents that we essentially were living in *The Amityville Horror*. The house was reportedly haunted, and since that movie was still fresh on everyone's mind, that was how they related to the house – via a movie. It couldn't be farther from the truth.

My mother recounted the events of the discovery of the house being haunted by saying:

One sunny day, a neighbor stopped me outside to say hello. She and her parents had lived next door for years. She seemed excited to tell me about our new home. It seemed that our house was a funeral parlor about 50 years earlier. Those convenient wide shelves in the basement were actually slabs where they prepared the bodies. (No one had mentioned that when we signed the lease.) Worse yet, she compared it to *The Amityville Horror*. She said "things happened" in the house. This news was unbelievable. I was too scared to ask "what things." I didn't want to hear it. I am one of those people who never had a desire to have a personal experience with anything other than worldly. How could that be right when I perceived the atmosphere of this home to be warm and friendly?

The next day, I had more unexpected company. The previous renter stopped by to see if she had any mail. I told her what the neighbor had revealed, comparing the house to Amityville. I anticipated her to call the neighbor crazy. My expectations were dashed when she agreed. This was too much to comprehend. I was horrified. This house had to be all right. With a new job, and little money, our family had to stay. There were no options.

My mother kept this knowledge to herself. She did not want me or my brother and sister to know what the neighbors thought and what was supposedly happening in the house. Little did she know that it was just a matter of time before the house would make its life-lasting impression upon me. It was very soon after moving into the house that I came to know the spirits firsthand, not just in my waking moments, but in my subconscious as well.

Back to the House

It was just a matter of time before we started hearing closets and the refrigerator opening and closing, and curtains being pulled back and opening on their own. Then shortly thereafter, I began hearing footsteps walking up and down the stairs and hallway.

The worst of it came in the middle of the night when I would awaken to find a strange man standing in my doorway that was threatening to enter the room. Oftentimes when this happened, I was struck with such an overwhelming fear that I could not move or say anything. I would sit up in bed and stare as this strange man stood there watching me. After a few minutes, he would disappear right before my eyes and I would lie down and go back to sleep as though nothing ever happened. I never said anything to my family about the events that started happening; for whatever reason, I kept it to myself.

The basement of the house was the most intriguing. It was unfinished, with a concrete floor and concrete slab shelves that lined the basement walls. My brother, sister, and I would roller skate and play there all the time. I used the shelves to put my STAR WARS® toys on and set up little dioramas with the figures and ships. Later, we would come to find out that the concrete slabs were used for something else entirely. My mother tells more of her discovery:

Although basements gave me the creeps, and I couldn't watch scary movies without getting night fears, as a parent, it was my responsibility to be brave. So I totally suppressed any thoughts of possible paranormal forces residing with us.

My mother had her own thoughts on the experiences and how she handled them being a young mother of three children:

The first time I found the refrigerator door open, I thought maybe I didn't shut it properly. After that, I made sure the door was shut, tight and secured. Even if I hadn't gone near the refrigerator, I would turn around from the sink and there it stood open a foot or two. Moments before, it was closed. I saw it closed; I'd glance back and it was open. This would happen several times in one day, then not happen for a week for two.

Moms with three kids spend a lot of time in the kitchen. Oddly enough, I became accustomed to finding the refrigerator door open. With my history as one of the walking spooked, I don't know why this didn't scare me. The atmosphere in the house still felt friendly. In retrospect, it felt a lot like you would feel if one of your kids played a prank on you. I would shake my head and smile – an odd response from me.

I am sure that there are skeptics who can explain why the refrigerator door appeared to open by itself, but I doubt that they can explain the kitchen curtains. These were the typical kitchen curtains with the top seam that allows them to be threaded on a rod. I'm not sure how soon after I first found the refrigerator door opened that I found the curtains open. They covered a window that had been painted shut many years ago, so no breeze caused this movement. In fact, they were moved back from the top of the rod like an unseen hand had reached up to the rod and pushed the curtains over to the left about eighteen inches.

Some days I found the curtains *and* the refrigerator door open. Other times I found closet doors or bedroom doors open. Some days I felt like I wasn't alone. Still, I never felt scared or felt that my family was in danger. I don't know what unseen agent teased us. Like Amityville? No, not at all. Not for us. Perhaps it is the family who influences the house, rather than the house that influences the family. After a year in Dover, circumstances brought us back to Wilmington. Since that time, I never felt such amity in a new home. My memories of our stay in Dover are always warmhearted and happy.

I never shared my account of the Dover house with my children until many years later. At the time, I didn't want to scare them. They never seemed affected by the house. However, I was wrong.

Yes, I was affected by the house. This is where it would all begin for me. My first paranormal experiences, th first experiences that opened me up to the possibility of all these supernatural occurrences and pursuits.

Over the summer of 2011, my sister and I went to Dover as she helped me gather photos for the book. We drove to our old house and parked in the church parking lot next to it.

"I am going to go knock on the door. What's the worst that could happen?" I said.

I got out of the car and put my camera on the front seat. I looked at my sister, closed the door, and made my way to the front porch, up the steps and to the front door. I knocked hard four times. In the background, a dog began to bark as I heard stirring coming from inside. Slowly, the door began to open and there was a kind-looking, elderly man at the door.

"Can I help you?" he asked politely.

"Um, yes..." I muttered. "I am an author writing a book on Delaware and my family lived in this house many years ago. I wanted to come by and see the house and hoped to talk to the residents."

We proceeded to talk for a few more moments and he asked my family name. It turns out that he was the original owner of the house and shortly after we moved out, he and his family moved in. He was open to the idea of us coming inside the house to look around. I motioned to my sister and she joined me on the front steps.

The elderly man welcomed us into the house. I was overrun with excitement. I never thought that I would actually step inside the house once more. We entered to find his wife sitting in a recliner, knitting. A little dog ran about our feet and barked as he tried to figure out who we were. It was like a wave that came over me as the feelings and memories of our time living in the house overtook me. My sister and I talked with them for about twenty minutes. We talked about our families and the changes to the house over the years. Surprisingly, not much had actually changed except for the carpets and the color of the house on the outside.

I did not disclose that our visit was one motivated by the paranormal. It didn't seem to be the right topic of discussion. I was just happy to enter the house and see it one more time. It was a great experience that helped to spark the memories of the good times that my family had in that house. Yes, there was paranormal activity too, but it was our home and one that we loved even though we were there for such a short time.

A haunted house is still a house and a home for the families who live in them. Despite that, at times things can scare us or be unsettling; it is, after all, still our home. My family had many experiences in that house, and it goes without saying that I would not be on the path I am now in the realm of paranormal research, investigations, and writing, if it were not for the events and experiences that I had while living there. Because of this knowledge and experience, I have made it a part of my "mission" as an investigator to help families and individuals, to help them understand and know that what they are experiencing is something special and not something to be afraid of.

The Dream

I can't say for certain when exactly it started, but not too long after we moved into the Dover house, I started having a recurring dream. The dream started when I was 5 and stayed with me until I was about 13 years old. As I grew, the dream became less frequent; but to this day, I can vividly remember every detail. This is the dream.

It began with me sitting by the window of a vehicle. It was similar to a bus or train car. There were rows of seats and windows, but what made it strange was that I could see the earth beneath me, the sky above and everything in front. There wasn't any ground beneath me. The vehicle seemed to be floating or flying as it moved fast through the atmosphere. There were bright mists and clouds that surrounded the vehicle on all sides. The vehicle moved so quickly that the clouds swirled by me in a stream of colors and patterns.

There were "beings" or "spirits" flying alongside the vehicle. They had a torso with a head and arms, but they ended in a point, or tail, and had no lower extremities. They danced and intertwined with each other as they flew alongside me.

Up ahead of us, we were moving towards a mountain, or a type of pyramid shape. The spirits and energy all seemed to be converging on this point. I knew that this was where we were headed and that we were to become part of the energy going into this terrain. Everything moved in "fast forward" and I felt like I was continuously trying to catch my breath. The trip was a thrill and a scare at the same time.

In this dream, I never made it to the destination. I would always wake up before getting there. The frequency of this dream was at least several times a week and became less frequent with time. Still, it remained intact from start to finish.

I can still close my eyes and relive the dream in its entirety to this day. I don't think the words I used to describe it really do it justice. I have tried to interpret it in several ways, but it is all too strange to really understand its meaning. My spiritualist friends interpret it as a spiritual journey or an astral voyage through some other plane of existence. I can't say for certain, but I know that it was otherworldly.

Despite the dream, the man in the doorway, and the other things that happened in the house, it still remained a house that was very warm and welcoming and I still think of the house fondly.

The impact of that dream has lasted all of my days. I was too young to fully understand or comprehend its meaning and what exactly it was that I was experiencing. It is a commonly shared belief that dreams are a portal where two worlds collide; the living and the dead can meet here, communicate, and share experiences. Spirits can challenge the living, or simply, the living goes into a world beyond their own. This is the betwixt and between; the neverending twilight where we can experience things beyond our own realities.

Dover – Quick Haunts

THE BLUE COAT INN
There are two spirits that are reported to haunt these grounds. The spirit of an old man has been seen lurking about, and the spirit of a young boy who appears to be a drummer boy is also seen on this premises.

DICKINSON MANSION
The ghost of John Dickinson is reported to haunt his dwelling. Other reports include phantom sounds and disembodied voices.

John Dickinson Home, from the side, just outside the fence.

THE GOVERNOR'S MANSION

There are several ghosts that have been reported at this location. The ghost of a gentleman from the eighteenth century that has a certain propensity for emptying wine glasses left in precarious positions. There is also the spirit of a lost soul who is heard to be rattling chains coming from the basement, where the Underground Railroad once passed. The spirit of a little girl in a red dress can be seen playing in the gardens.

Outside the Governor's House, in the heart of downtown Dover.

THE GREEN AT DOVER

The spirit of an angry judge looking for justice reportedly walks the grounds near where the supreme court of Delaware is located.

On the green, where the spirit of an angry judge roams the land. In the background is the Supreme Court of Delaware building.

The Green, Dover, Delaware

BLACK DIAMOND ROAD – SMYRNA

The urban legend of Black Diamond Road in Smyrna, Delaware has all the makings of what could be a great horror movie. The land is purportedly a former Native American burial site, and the spirits of these same people are seen in the neighboring fields and areas along the road. There are reports of glowing lights seen from the road – a glimpse of ghost torches and fires? It is reported that the residents in the development adjacent to the road take picture upon picture that reveal remnants of these native spirits.

I have no doubts about the possibility of the land being a native burial ground. Delaware is known for them from north to south and east to west. In fact, I recall as a child visiting a site in South Bowers Beach where you could see the unearthed remains of the native burial ground. Since then the museum/site has been filled-in out of respect for these ancestors and for their living descendants.

View along Black
Diamond Road.

View along Black
Diamond Road.

In the neighborhood along
Black Diamond Road.

NORTH UNION STREET – SMYRNA

I found several accounts about the spirit of a girl in a white dress being seen in houses somewhere on North Union Street, Smyrna. As well, there were reports of furniture being moved, objects taken or disappearing, and electrical appliances and lights turning on and off. These conditions are a recurring theme in the typical "Classic Haunting" or "Residual Haunting" that often occurs in private haunted homes. However, this information did not supply a specific home or homes where the activity was taking place. I was able to pinpoint the general area to North Union Street in Smyrna based upon several different descriptions and accounts, but still was unable to determine exactly where on this street this activity occurred.

North Union Street, where the apparition of
a girl in white is seen roaming the land.

TALKING BOARDS

The modern spiritualist movement began with two sisters in the year 1848, with Margaret and Kate Fox in a little cabin in New York State. The concept of spirit communication began as they came up with interesting ways to speak with the spirit world.

It began with "table tipping." This method used letters from the alphabet. The table would turn, topple, or fall over when the correct letter was called. The approach was to use the table as a planchette, where those involved would lightly place their fingertips on the edge of the table.

The next spirit communication device consisted of a pencil attached to one end of a small basket. The medium would touch the basket to initiate contact with the spirit realm and the messages would be written on a piece of paper. The pencil basket would evolve into the more modern-day planchette, which was heart-shaped and consisted of two rotating castors and a pencil at the tip.

The exact moment when the modern-day talking board came about is unknown, but an article published in a spiritualist quarterly review in 1871 clearly talks about the use of a pointing device and cards used to display the alphabet for deciphering the cryptic messages from beyond.

In the March 28, 1886 issue of *American Spiritualist Magazine* is the first mentioning of a spirit communication device as a "Talking Board." The first patent was granted on February 10, 1891, to inventor Elijah J. Bond and lists Charles W. Kennard and William H. A. Maupin as co-inventors of the new message board. Whether or not they are the actual inventors or capitalists that took advantage of an idea is yet to be known, but they were the first to market the board as a novelty item or board game.

The origination of OUIJA® came about when co-inventor Charles Kennard performed a session with Elijah Bonds' sister-in-law, where they asked of the board to provide a name that they could use to market and sell it under. The board spelled out O-U-I-J-A, and when Charles asked the meaning of the name, it spelled "Good Luck." Elijah's sister-in-law then revealed a locket in her possession that had the name OUIJA spelled on it. Almost immediately the board was marketed and sold as "The Ouija."

Through the following decades there would be many incarnations of the "Talking Board," as many novelty and toy companies came out with their own brand of the popular spirit device. In the 1940s is when the "Talking Board" was at its most popular. There were versions that had everything from genies to cannibals depicted on the boards, and everything in between.

In modern time, Parker Brothers is the sole survivor of the talking board era, and to this day the talking board is synonymous with the word OUIJA.

Talking Board Obsession

My family had only lived in the Dover house for one year, but the experiences that I had in that house were so profound that they would affect me for the rest of my life. I know without them I would not be where I am now as a writer, investigator, and researcher of the paranormal. It wouldn't be until a few years after the Dover house that I would have my next paranormal experiences. No one could know that these experiences would shape and define my direction, and eventual obsession, with certain things within the paranormal.

After we left the Dover house, we moved back into the Wilmington area, where we lived in another house for only one year. My younger brother, Luke, was born while we lived at that house. We moved on from there to the house in Newark where I would stay until I graduated high school and left home for the first time at seventeen in pursuit of a music career.

Sixth grade restarted the paranormal. At 11 years old, I was still frightened of my own shadow, yet somehow I managed to get involved with friends in the world of spirit communication.

I am going to call one of the principal characters Sam.

Sam was a friend whose family's history with the paranormal got intertwined with mine as our friendship continued through sixth grade. We were only friends for that one school year; after that we went on to different schools.

Sam's influence amongst our friends was great and profound. He was charismatic, full of energy, and all of us who knew him liked him. I was still a very shy and awkward boy who was full of social inabilities and insecurities. I was happy to *have* friends and feel like I could be a part of something. I didn't really have enough personality to be the voice of reason or confrontation when it was needed. I simply went along with what everyone else was doing, and because of that, it made me vulnerable and easily influenced.

How Sam and I became friends I cannot really say, but we did and spent our time during lunch, recess, and after school involved in the things that we liked; and for a time, what we liked the most was using a talking board to communicate with the spirits of the dead.

I can remember the first time that we used the board. It was a sleepover at Sam's house with several of our friends. We were in the basement's den and had just finished watching some *James Bond* movies when Sam disappeared for a moment and returned with the board. I had never seen such a thing.

The board was made by someone in his family. It was a large rectangular piece of wood that was about an inch thick and stained a dark color. The letters, numbers, and *yes-no-maybe* were burned into the wood and then smoothed over with a finish that made the board reflective and shiny at times. He put the board on a coffee table in front of us and we all crowded around it, sitting on the floor. Sam explained how the board worked and what we would do to try to communicate with ghosts or spirits.

I was apprehensive of what we were about to do. I had distinct memories of the spirit things that happened to me when I was younger and was still battling with the dream that had haunted me in Dover. I was unsettled with the idea of participating, but did not have the courage to say *no*.

An upside-down shot glass was the planchette. He put the shot glass on the table and we all put our fingers on the glass as Sam instructed.

"Are there any ghosts here?" Sam asked with a tone of confidence in his voice.

My fingers were poised on the glass along with my friends. I watched the glass intensely and waited for something to happen. The glass did not move.

"We want to talk to you! Are you here?" Sam asked again.

My gaze was still focused on the glass. I watched and waited for the glass. You must keep the tips of your fingers lightly touching the glass. No direct pressure. Allow yourself to be a conduit of energy that the spirits can use to manipulate the glass in responce to the questions.

I was new to this whole concept and was not sure of what would happen or how. All I knew was that fear had already begun to grow inside me. We waited in silence after Sam asked the question again. The lights were dim in the room and the rest of the house was quiet, as it was well after midnight. Sam looked up from the glass at all of us. I felt nervous as he looked at me and then turned his attention back to the board. My eyes followed his as I looked at our fingers touching the glass.

"Where are you? Will you talk to us?" Sam asked again, but now with a sense of defiance and frustration in his voice. It was subtle at first, but then slowly, but surely, you could feel a vibration coming up through the board and into the glass. It was like a buzzing that reached the tips of our fingers. I wasn't sure if what was happening was supposed to happen.

The glass started to move sluggishly at first as though it was being dragged across the board. My initial instinct was that Sam was playing a trick on us and manipulating the glass under his control. The glass inched its way over and stopped on "Yes" as a response to our question. Sam then pulled the glass back to center and asked another question.

"What is your name?" The glass started to move again, and this time, it was moving towards individual letters to spell out a name. The glass moved slowly, but much more fluidly towards the first letter H, then off to the second A, the third R, the fourth R, and the last Y. Harry.

The sense of dread was growing, evolving to fear. Even though this name seemed unassuming and non-threatening, I did not like the fact that we were communicating with something.

"Oh, hi, Harry. It's nice to talk to you again!" Sam spoke with excitement and energy. "This is my friend Harry. I have talked to him many times before," Sam explained.

I was uncomfortable, but continued on because I only had little-boy choices. I could either go along with it and everything would be fine or I could chicken out and face ridicule for the rest of that night, and probably for weeks to come at school. I opted for the first choice. It seemed like the easier of the two.

As the night wore on, we continued talking to "Harry." I became less fearful and more interested in what "he" had to say. The glass was moving much quicker now as Harry answered each question and seemed to be gaining energy and speed. We must have talked to Harry for about an hour and eventually called it a night.

The following Monday in school, Sam was not there. He apparently was out sick, and, as I soon realized, he missed school more frequently than most of my classmates. I wouldn't see Sam again until Tuesday at lunch in the cafeteria.

Sam came over to our table and sat down. I was with the same group of friends that had been at his house on that previous Saturday.

"Hey guys," Sam said as he sat down with his lunch tray.

"Hi Sam; where you been?" one of my other friends asked.

"Oh, I was home sick with a stomach flu. Yeah, after you guys left on Sunday morning, I got really sick and couldn't get out of bed for the rest of the weekend and into Monday," Sam said in a straight, matter-of-fact way.

"Oh. How are you feeling now?" my other friend asked.

"I am fine and feeling better now!" Sam replied. We ate lunch and talked about what normal 11 year olds do, or at least for us; we talked about Sci-Fi movies, James Bond and, of course, we talked about Harry.

We had all finished eating with plenty of time to spare during our lunch break and still had about ten minutes before recess.

"Hey, you guys want to try and talk to Harry?" Sam asked as he looked at each of us one at a time.

"Umm, okay," I replied.

"Okay, do any of you have a quarter and a piece of loose leaf paper?" Sam asked.

"I do," said a friend. He reached into his backpack and pulled out the paper and dug into his pocket to retrieve the quarter. Sam drew on the paper the numbers, letters and Yes-No-Maybe in the same fashion as was on his talking board that we used at his house.

"Okay guys, put a finger on the edge of the quarter like we did on the glass," Sam said as he demonstrated with his own finger on what we should do. We all placed our fingers on the quarter. Sam asked his first question.

"Harry, are you here?"

The creep-out factor that I had felt at Sam's house was not present since it was the middle of the day, at school, in the cafeteria surrounded by other fourth, fifth, and sixth graders.

The quarter remained still for a moment, then slowly started to move and settled over the word "Yes."

Sam moved the quarter back to center and asked his next question.

"Harry, can you see us?"

The quarter started to move faster and slid over to "yes" again. We only got to ask a few more questions before lunch was over. Sam picked up the piece of paper, crumpled it up, and threw it in the trash as we went outside to recess. For the next half hour, we ran and played like normal sixth graders should have as we quickly shed off the paranormal encounter. It did not scare me as it had just a few days before. I was starting to think about my own questions for Harry and wonder who Harry really was.

The rest of the day in school I was distracted, as I found my mind wandering back to the talking board and the session that we had on that Saturday night at Sam's house. Fortunately, I would go through the day unnoticed and none of my teachers called on me for answers to any of their questions. Otherwise, I would have been caught in a daydream which always ended up making me look silly and drew unnecessary attention from my classmates.

Over the next few weeks, the obsession grew. We found ourselves eating our lunches faster and faster so that we could spend as much time as possible talking to Harry.

The next sleepover at Sam's turned into a night of the talking board as we spent little time doing anything else. Other spirits were starting to come forward, and we found ourselves talking to more than one as the night pushed on. We must have talked to at least three or four different spirits that night and had received all kinds of information about them. My fear had grown into confidence, obsession, and I found myself asking questions throughout the sessions, too. Sam and I would take turns going back and forth asking questions while our other friends in attendance would participate, but say nothing.

Sam and I became closer friends as a result of the talking board and the daily sessions that we conducted in the cafeteria at lunch time. We would also find ourselves talking to each other about it as much as we could in our classes whenever the teacher wasn't paying attention, or whenever any opportunity afforded us to do so. If there was any project or task that required us to partner up with someone, Sam and I were always the first to work together, because we knew it was an excuse for us to talk about Harry and the spirits.

Sam was beginning to share another family secret.

I remember very distinctly the first time that he showed me the "book." He kept it in his backpack and was secretive about showing it to me. He pulled it out of his bag from under the table and never brought it up on top of the desk. He feared the teacher seeing it and certainly did not want to have to explain what it was and what he was doing with it in the middle of class.

The book was a paperback, the size of a typical novel. It had a black cover with white lettering down the spine and on the cover. Beneath the title of the book on the cover was a circle with a series of symbols in it. The font of the title made the book even more ominous and with the name of It spread across the front and above the symbol it made it seem very powerful. *Necronomicon* was the name of the book.

This was the first time that this book would appear in my life, but certainly not the last. Sam explained that this was a book of black magic and spells, and that it was his brother's. He said that his brother had used it several times to perform some of the magic in the book, but that nothing really happened. As soon as I saw the book and Sam had explained what it was, I was afraid. I wanted no part of that book and I was so scared of it that I didn't even want to see it. It terrified me enough to keep me away. But Sam wouldn't hear of it.

He would speak about its contents in great detail and would flip to certain pages in the book to show me the symbols and diagrams. I would look, but was always squeamish at the sight of the strange language, words, and symbols. This book was also known as the *Book of the Dead*, and the sense of power that came from this book was enough to disturb me and send chills through my veins any time Sam mentioned it or dared to bring it out at school.

It was during this time that my interests in the paranormal grew tenfold. I remember that we would often get a catalogue from which we could order books and that all types of subjects and interests were available; everything from the Hardy Boys to those infamous "Choose Your Own Adventures" and others. I came across books on ghosts stories and there was even a book on numerology that I ordered and became engrossed in. I was becoming more and more interested in ghosts and spirits, but still kept away from the book that Sam carried with him at all times.

It was subtle at first, but the sessions with the talking board became darker and darker. I made my own talking board using the piece of paper and quarter like we used at school. I ran my own sessions at my own sleepovers in my house. The spirits that started to come through and communicate with us began to predict our futures. I remember it telling me specifically how I was going to fail in school and get bad grades. I rebelled against the idea because I knew I was a decent student and that that was never going to happen.

The names of the spirits were more obscure and darker as well. Some of these names should never be mentioned since it can give the entities power. But one name that came through that I knew was a total lie was *Jesus*.

The first time that this name came through, I knew immediately that the spirit was being deceitful. My Catholic, Christian upbringing along with CCD (A church night school that prepped us for our first communion, confession, and confirmation) was enough to tell me that Jesus would not be coming through a talking board to speak to us. The very idea of that still gives me chills, knowing how deceptive and dark this spirit was that it would pretend to be the messiah. This spirit that took on that holy name was the same one that continued to say awful things to us and make dire predictions. This was the spirit that I would communicate with on my own quite frequently. My bond with the spirit realm via these talking boards became so strong that it wouldn't take more than the first question before the board was responding with the same energy that took twenty questions on the first night.

Sam continued to bring up the book every chance he got. Even though he wore my resistance down, I still refused to touch it or hold it in my hands. I wanted nothing to do with it and at that time knew to leave it alone.

We had several more sleepovers and many more sessions with the talking board, but it all came to a screeching halt on one particular night at Sam's house.

It was late, and we were well into the session with the board. Harry had been talking with us off and on throughout the night as well as my spirit that had been communicating with me on my own. At this point, despite my obsession and interest in the board and sessions, I began to feel uneasy and unsettled. It was not unlike how I felt on the *first* night that we conducted a session.

The continued information and predictions that the spirits had been giving us over the past several months had built up to the point that I found myself more concerned about what they had to say than anything else. It would be the same stuff that would keep me up at night and often would be the subject of my dreams. I found myself waking up at all hours of the night in fear and panic as my dreams disturbed me and scared me out of my wits. Unfortunately, I cannot remember the exact details of the dreams, but only the feelings that they left me with, which haunt me to this day. We were several hours into our session. We had taken several breaks throughout the night, but we stayed at it until the moment when the unexpected happened.

Sam was getting agitated with the board as the spirit we were communicating with began to be difficult and give us nonsensical answers. Several times, the glass would simply start to move in circles in the middle of the board and slowly start to pick up speed as it spun round and round. Sam had to stop it several times and bring it back to center in attempts to try and start again. The spirit would answer the first question or two, but then the glass would go back into moving in circles about the board.

"Why aren't you answering me?" Sam demanded of the board. The glass continued to move in circles. "Harry, where are you? Why won't you speak to us anymore?" Sam asked again. The glass continued as before. "You better answer us! We want to speak to you! Harry?" Sam asked.

We watched in amazement and fear as the glass continued to move in circles about the board. The glass began to pick up speed and the vibration coming from the board through the glass was starting to be felt by everyone who touched it. Suddenly, the glass started to heat up as though it was sitting on some hot surface that was now heating the glass. The spinning glass sped up. It was clear that whomever or whatever we were talking to was becoming angry with us as well. Our other friends dropped off the glass and backed away as fear and panic began to set about the room. Sam and I remained on the glass as it continued to move faster and faster in circles. Our other two friends retreated away from the board and moved off to the side of the room, near the stairwell that lead up to the kitchen. The both of them had become visibly disturbed. They were not as committed as Sam and I.

Even though I kept my finger on the glass, I too began to become frightened. The dread was consuming, as nerves began to take hold.

"SAM!" I cried out.

"What?" Sam replied.

"What do we do?" I asked.

"I don't know, but keep your finger on the glass!" Sam demanded.

"I don't want to! I want to stop! Please!" I begged Sam.

Meanwhile, our other two friends moved closer to the stairwell as they prepared to flee.

"Harry! Make this stop! I command you!" Sam spoke out defiantly.

"Sam, what is happening?" I asked again. My voice began to quiver as I tried to choke down the fear inside me. The glass was hot under our fingertips, but not so hot that we thought we were going to get burned. The glass was moving in circles at such a pace that it was clear that it was not either one of us manipulating it for the sake of a dramatic effect. The glass picked up speed yet again, and before Sam or I could react, the glass shot out from under our fingers and flew across the room. It smashed into the wall into million little pieces!

That was enough! Before anyone could react further, we all scattered and pushed each other out of the way as we scrambled to get up the stairs and out of the room. Even Sam, regardless of his best efforts, was stricken with fear!

Despite all the commotion that we were making in the kitchen, not one of his parents or siblings woke up and came down to see what all the racket was about.

Sam was the first to regain his composure and instantly began talking us all down off our prospective ledges. I was shaking, did *not* want to go back down into the basement den. Sam suddenly became angry and commanded us back down into the basement. We were all too scared to fight back or do otherwise, so we returned to the den. Sam began to clean up the mess that the glass made after it smashed into the wall. We all moved our sleeping bags off to one side of the room and as far away from that wall as we could. It was as if we thought the wall was going to reach out and grab us, when in actuality it was the talking board that we should have been frightened of.

Sam then took the board upstairs. He came back downstairs and told us to go to sleep. I don't think that I slept much, if any, that night. I remember pulling the sleeping bag up over my head and I hid inside of it like it was a cocoon protecting me from all the potentially bad things that lay just beyond its protective covering. It was my shield of armor, as though this was really going to stop any ghosts or spirits from getting me; but the rationale of a frightened 11 year old will create anything to bring comfort and shove away the fear.

The next day, Sam woke up and acted as if nothing had happened. The rest of us were still too shaken to want to acknowledge what had occurred. In the back of our minds, we were all grateful to have made it through the night without any further incident.

That night would be the last sleepover at Sam's house. Our friendship, after that, would never be the same, as I had vowed that I would never participate in a talking board session again! I wanted no further part in any activity of the sort and I certainly did not want to see that book that Sam made me view at every opportunity. The fear stayed with me for months after that night, and the nightmares that would come would frighten me so much that oftentimes I'd wake up crying or screaming from the terror that lay behind my eyes, deep in my subconscious.

Little did I know, that this would only be the beginning of a chapter in my life where the book that Sam had would make its appearance again, as well as the dark spirits that began to frequent us during our latter sessions with the board. The sign of things yet to come was written on the wall, but I did not have the foresight to read it.

Newark – A Hamlet's History

Newark's early settlements are a historical mystery. There are too few records for definitive answers. But mainstream historians make a best guess that, in the early 1700s, the little English, Welsh, and Scots-Irish village developed on top of a couple native trails. As the talk of revolution grew louder amongst the dissatisfied colonists, traffic grew heavier between Virginia and Maryland, and Philadelphia through little Newark. Catering to these travelers became an important merchant trade. Various mills, such as saw and grist popped up along the local White Clay and Christina Creeks to supply needed wood for building and grain to eat. Rich soil for crops and local ore from Iron Hill added to the trades of tanning and brick making, which established Newark as a new, bustling and upcoming community. Newark was officially born in 1758 with a charter issued by King George II. In 1765, a small grammar school had moved to Newark, renaming itself the Newark Academy, and prospered quietly in the years leading to the Revolution. Today, that little school has graduated into the big leagues and is now the University of Delaware.

During the Second World and Korean Wars, Newark was enriched by swift commercial and industrial increases. The DuPont Company opened several of its manufacturing and research plants in the town, and by 1951, Chrysler Corporation built the high-tech Newark Assembly car plant. The state government in Dover wrote a new charter for the town, doubling its size.

THE REAL ESTATE GAMBIT

We were invited into Elaine's current piece of real estate. It was a nice townhouse sitting in Newark, Delaware. The modern interior hosted smidgens of the eclectic. A small, four-seat dinette in the dining area sported two huge candles that resembled a gateway to some holy of holies rather than an interior design choice.

Elaine faced us with medium-length black hair, soft, deep eyes set in a round face, and a mouth that spoke tomes using few words. Her very first memory as a child was of the supernatural. And from that first time forward she has been involved, aware, and perhaps, in control of many aspects of the infinite. As she told her story, one began to sense a mighty individual with an untainted, precise spiritual awareness. While clearly the captain of her life-ship, she appears at ease with treating the crew as equals. While the bulk of us are taught from childhood that only the physical world has any worth, Elaine's mother, a sensitive, taught her daughter how to stay afloat on the many waves of reality. And while she makes use of her intuitive powers daily, she is modest, keeping her real energy locked in the strong-room of her deeper spiritual self.

But even Elaine couldn't foresee how the spirit realm would funnel her and her family to a particular house when she moved to Delaware fourteen years ago. I'm sure, to Elaine, the following story fit well into the criteria of *Ghosts of Delaware*. To the interviewer, it felt apparent that this tale was only one grain of sand on the Elaine-beach of fantastic paranormal adventures.

"I moved to Delaware from California in 1997, with my then-husband Francis and my 1-year-old son, who is now fifteen. We were staying with my best friend and her family, living in their finished basement, in Newark,

Delaware. We wanted to buy a house. A realtor was engaged and she took us to see, in the end, a dozen homes. Of those twelve, three made house hunting a pretty wild time.

One of the first properties our lady realtor showed us was on Porter Road in Newark. It was the development where the original farmhouse was left standing near the entrance, a token of country times. We walked through the downstairs, from the living room to the kitchen, and it wasn't a bad property, but it needed work. On the second floor, we made our way through the bedrooms and baths. All seemed fine.

Last was the attic. Up the steps we climbed to face a small window at the top. On the left was a door to a finished office area with steep gabled ceilings, fresh paint on new drywall, and wall-to-wall carpet. On the right of the staircase was another door.

"There's nothing finished in that space," the realtor said. "It's just storage."

My husband was carrying our son and wasn't interested in seeing a grimy, unfinished attic. He followed the realtor down the steps to the first floor.

My curiosity demanded that I see the entire house. I grabbed the knob and shoved the creaky door open. Up along the rafters, on both sides of the room, were these huge masses of ... something. They looked like big mushy balloons, solid in appearance, yet not balloons. The room was surprisingly cold compared to the rest of the house and even outside. Then the two masses began to move, in and out, like lungs. I could hear those things inhaling large amounts of air and then exhaling them with a slow *whoosh*.

I froze in place. What was I to make of this? I'd never seen anything so bizarre and out of place, and I've seen many strange things in my life.

Then a voice spoke, gravelly and deep. "Get out!" The lungs were feeding the words. "Get out!"

A second warning was not necessary. I spun around, ran out, slammed the door, flew down the steps, grabbed my husband and my son, and said, "We're getting outa here!"

"What's wrong?" the realtor asked, as if I was being chased by a monster rat.

"We gotta go. There are two giant lungs in the attic," I explained as if she'd understand. "And they told me to get out."

"What?!" the lady exclaimed.

I couldn't explain further.

We hurried into the car, and as my husband backed out of the driveway, I glanced at the attic window. A "lung" was still visible, breathing away anyone it didn't like.

A few days after the "lung" house, our realtor took us to see the George Penny House, a historical home on Philadelphia Pike in Claymont, Delaware. You can look up the Penny House on the Internet. It has a lot of history. There are several ghost stories tied to it. It was formally a brothel. George Washington slept there. Lafayette slept there; seems like everyone slept there.

I loved this house.

We were all upstairs checking out the place. My little boy was toddling around from bedroom to bedroom, having a good time. I was following him to keep him out of trouble. We went into one of the bedrooms, where he suddenly stopped and turned to me.

"I want this bedroom," he said in his *babyfied*, 1-year-old way. He had begun talking very early compared to most children.

"Oh, okay," I replied with pride. My son knows what he likes.

Instantly, my eyes filled with a horrid scene. It was a vision. My son was being pushed out a window in this bedroom by a little girl. My blood turned to water ice.

Just then the baby started towards the window.

And out of nowhere, the ghost of a little girl appeared. She was about the size of a 4-year old, wearing a pinafore with a tie in the back, and had blonde hair. Only her back was visible from where I stood. She was gliding towards the baby. I jumped towards him, took his hand and pulled him back away from the window.

"No! You are not going to push my son out the window!" I yelled at the little ghost. I took the baby and marched down the stairs.

Apparently, that was the girl's room and she wasn't into sharing. Because I loved the house so much, I wasn't going to let this pushy spook keep me from getting it. I was sure I could handle the little girl. She didn't scare me. If I just put on my "mom" voice, I'm sure, in time, she would learn to behave.

The baby and I joined my husband and the realtor, who were out back. The area was lovely, with an old spring house. There was also a pond nearby, but the weeds and overgrown plants made it look more like a bog. I felt an uneasiness about the pond.

"If we buy this place, we'll have to drain the pond. Otherwise, the baby could drown," I heard myself explain.

Then I glanced back to the house for a good view of the porch and the lovely shrubs around it. Above the porch roof, in the window of the bedroom we had just left, I saw the little ghost-girl staring down at us with her cute rounded face. But her eyes were black.

No matter. If the house hadn't needed so much electrical and plumbing work, we would have bought it! I explained all these reasons to the realtor as to why we wouldn't buy, including the little girl ghost. The realtor looked up to the second-floor windows, obviously saw nothing, then looked at me.

"Oh, you Californians," she said with an uneasy laugh. "You are so wacky!"

I could tell she wanted us to buy a house sooner rather than later, to get us off the streets.

A few days later, we had an appointment with the same realtor to see a house on Welsh Tract Road. It was a little private road, set back in the woods, with only a couple houses on it. My son was asleep in his car seat. Francis and I would take turns looking at the house while the other parent stayed in the car with the baby.

The car was parked off the street in the owner's driveway. With Francis in the house and the baby fast asleep in the back seat, I decided to take the short venture to the empty carport in front of our car and glance into the backyard. This was the twelfth property we had toured with the lady realtor.

The house sat on an acre of ground surrounded by woodlands. The property was on the back side of Ironhill, one of the few upward protrusions in the otherwise flat state of Delaware. The view was serene, peaceful, and beautiful. The sunny, early fall day painted the edges of the oaks and maples with highlights of reds and yellows.

All of a sudden, I see these people, these six men, in a staggered group, walking in the woods. I could see they were trudging, hunched over and moving slowly. They seemed to be struggling to move through the area.

I thought to myself, *What the heck have these guys been doing?* I took a few steps closer to the fence that separated the carport from the yard.

I was mesmerized. The men were all wearing horrid, ragged and torn Revolutionary War uniforms. Their faces were dirty. Their heads and feet were wrapped in bloody bandages. They were carrying antique muskets that looked brand new. Tired, exhausted, they appeared to be in pain or great distress, as if from a real battle. And each of their steps continued to look torturous.

Now I'd heard about re-enactors here in the east that performed various battles from the American Revolution. Perhaps these men were re-enactors. What did I know? I'm new to the area. Maybe they always grope their way through forests near people's backyards to keep the whole thing realistic. If so, they were doing Academy Award-winning jobs.

The fence gate in front of me was unlocked, so I pushed it open and strode quickly half way across the yard, closer to the woods, so that I could get a better look.

That's when I realized something. This scene, that had so entranced me, turned unreal.

One of the soldiers suddenly stopped, looked right at me with amazing blue eyes and said *"Thank God you're here. Now we can rest."*

With that, in unison, the six men began to fade away, as all six sunk straight down into the ground, like ships on a dirt-filled sea.

I immediately knew; we *have* to buy this house!"

And they did. The final push from the afterlife was successful in steering Elaine and her family to the house where they, spirit and human, would be most comfortable, most at ease. Throughout the twelve years she stayed on Welsh Tract Road, Elaine researched the area to learn anything she could about the military specters, but found naught. Although no longer physically connected to the area, Elaine still feels a magnetic attraction – to the soldiers. In her mind, she can still sit on the back deck of that house, and feel protected by the ghostly army lying in peace at the edge of the real estate.

Darkness Consumes...

High School – In the Beginning

High school for just about everyone I know was a difficult and trying time. I believe it is one of the most difficult transitions that one can face in their lives. We are moving from childhood into young adulthood, but high school seems to be stuck in between these stages.

I had just turned fourteen when I started high school. I was a bit behind in the puberty department, which made me feel extra awkward. My freshman year was probably the hardest of all, as I had to adjust to a new school. What made this transition difficult was the decision to switch from public school to an all-male Roman Catholic school instead. Not only was I not going to the school where my friends were going, but I had to take placement exams and all kinds of tests in order to be accepted and put into the proper level of classes. I tested well and I initially received a scholarship for part of my tuition that first year, as well as placement in advanced classes. It became abundantly clear though that, after my first semester, I was not happy in the school and completely disinterested in all that it had to offer. I had been a fairly decent student up to that point.

I had failed half of my classes after the first semester. Immediately, I lost the scholarship and went right onto academic probation. My parents were struggling to understand what was happening and I was upset by my own poor performance. It only added to the anxiety and stress that I was already experiencing from being at the school in the first place.

Here though is where the predictions of "Harry" and the other spirits of the talking board began to come true.

This was also the year that music took a great hold on me. I had been playing the violin since fourth grade. About halfway through eighth grade, I discovered the guitar and focused my attention on that. My grade school friend had also discovered music around that same time. We had lost touch being in different schools. If it hadn't been for the fact that we also lived in the same neighborhood we would have not been able to stay friends.

It was right after he learned that I played guitar that he asked me to join his Punk Rock band. Exposure to all types of music followed. It was an eye and ear opening experience as I discovered great music. Naturally, I started to spend more time with my friend and we hung out more and more as band members.

This childhood friend was a principal character in our "play of life" that was about to be staged.

Necronomicon – The Book of the Dead

We were in the bookstore at the mall when I came across the dreaded book *Necronomicon*. It was in the "New Age" section. I was drawn to it like a squirrel to peanuts, and immediately began to leaf through its pages.

I remembered all that Sam had told me about this book. I even remembered some of the symbols and words that he had shown me time and time again, but this time there was no fear. My curiosity was power-driven to know everything about its contents. I bought it without hesitation and began to consume it immediately.

The book was infectious as it absorbed all of my focus, energy, and concentration. I wanted nothing more than to read and understand this book. I was becoming like the "Mad Arab" Abdul Alhazred, who was the antagonist and focal point of the beginning of this dark grimoire.

The story of the *Necronomicon* begins with the "Mad Arab" as he combs the desert in the quest for knowledge of the dark arts. It is by chance that he happens upon the "summoning stone" with the magic symbols carved into it. He bears witness to the evil incantations being spout by the practitioners who danced and gave worship to the stone and the creature who began to emerge from beneath it. A portal of death and destruction was being unleashed upon the world as the creature rose from its depths. The guttural sounds of the "worshippers of the serpent" had reached their peak as the thing that "lay dreaming beneath the earth" awoke and rose from its slumber. The darkness and madness consumed the man and all that fell in the wake of the creature's wrath. This is how the stage is set for the tale of the "Mad Arab" and his own quest to gain the knowledge of the dark path and achieve the goals of moving through the gates of the Ancient Ones, and to the outer reaches of the deities that dwelled in the "un-zoned," a point beyond the stars.

The first few nights the book was never put down. It became my companion at school and anywhere that I could take it. It was read in every spare moment that I had. I was starting to understand the obsession that overtook Sam and why he would stay so attached to the book. The fear that the book instilled in its reader was enough to be able to quickly recognize the power it yielded and how dangerous it would be for the book to fall into the wrong hands. The incantations that the book described lead to the ultimate path to darkness, and once started, there was no retreat. My studies and concentration at school began to collapse even more as I dove deeper into the book. It consumed me. The contents of the book were written in my own words so that I could commit them to memory. The three core symbols that were on the cover of the book, as well as described on the "summoning stone," I drew over and over.

My second semester of my freshman year was worse than my first. The growing concern of my teachers and parents was for my physical and emotional good health. They had no clue the cause was metaphysical.

"The Cemetery Romp"

My experiences with the paranormal started at a young age. My investigations began at an early age, too. Of course, in my youth, the proper protocols or procedures were not followed or even conceived of. The only equipment that I had was an old VHS-C camcorder and a powerful curiosity for anything paranormal.

This particular experience would greatly influence my views and opinions on investigating cemeteries. It wasn't until many years later when I would actively go to a cemetery for paranormal purposes. It was during the time that Katharine Driver (then Sarro, my wife) was writing *Philadelphia Haunts* that we went to visit Mount Moriah Cemetery in Philadelphia, because of a tale told to us by our editor's husband. He had recounted an experience that he had as a teenager that was eerily similar to this one.

I was only 15. My Punk Rocker friends and band mates at the time decided it would be fun to go to an old cemetery just outside of Newark. I reluctantly agreed to go, but I really didn't have a choice. I didn't have a car. I didn't even have a license. So, I was at the mercy of my friends and had to play to the whims of their fancies.

I had already developed a keen sense of certain types of paranormal energies by this time. I have always had a leaning towards the darker, negative things, as far as how I would react to them and know that they were present.

It was a spring Saturday night and we were rapidly approaching our curfews. The leader of my group of friends led the charge as we made our way into the cemetery. It was almost immediately that a heaviness began in the pit of my stomach, crept up my spine, and slowly consumed my whole upper being. The pressure in my head felt very similar to having impacted sinuses or a borderline migraine headache. My friends ran on ahead without fear. They were living the "Punk Rock lifestyle," or at least as much one could at 16 years old. I was the conservative; I had to be clean shaven and my hair neatly cut. My high school was all male Roman Catholic; there would be no getting away with looking like a Punk Rocker.

So, there I stood at the edge of the cemetery. My friends abandoned me, running off in various directions into the cemetery. I was overwhelmed by the familiar unwelcome pressure. My senses were deluged by a feeling of dread and nausea from something that was lurking about.

In the distance, one of my friends called to me, but I remained still, not able to step forward into the cemetery. I knew that they would never let me live it down if I did not enter, and there was no way to explain what it was that I was feeling. At that time, the daily paranormal experiences I had were my secret and my burden to carry. I did not share with my friends or my family. For some, this story now will be the first airing of these experiences.

I took a deep breath, held it, and closed my eyes. I stepped into the cemetery; then another step, yet another. My eyes were still closed and I don't believe I had taken a breath yet, either! I walked forward blindly into a cemetery that I wanted no part of. The despair and ill feeling did not subside and only intensified with each step.

Then I opened my eyes; I was standing in front of a tombstone. The tombstone was sunken into the ground and leaned left. A part of it had broken off and was lying nearby. I looked at the tombstone from base to top.

When I looked beyond the tombstone, I saw it standing in front of me.

I was at a loss for words to describe it. It wasn't human, nor was it animal. It was some type of hybrid, twisted creature that stepped out of an H.P. Lovecraft story and into my reality. Looking back now, and trying to put it all into perspective, it made sense that it appeared to me in the form that it did. My beliefs at the time lent itself to these types of creatures and monsters that lurked in the shadows. This creature was not fully manifested, as parts of it had a certain transparency that made it a black cloud/mist. At times there were features that could be made out, but then it would shift out of focus like a dramatic zoom on a camera. It moved in and out of the physical realm and the visual one, too. I was dumbfounded, pierced with fear. I began to recoil in horror and stepped backwards. I did not want to turn away from this thing and take my eyes off it. There was no trust. I knew that as soon as I did, it would lunge!

I tripped over a piece of a tombstone, flew backwards, and landed flat on my back. It happened so fast that I was dazed, with the wind knocked out of me.

I picked my head up to see what the creature was doing. It was gone! It had vanished in just seconds.

I sat up, caught my breath, and frantically looked around. I knew it was still there. I was certain of it. *Where the hell are my friends?* I screamed to myself.

Up on my feet, I brushed myself off, but never looked away from my surroundings. This thing was lurking about and I was waiting for it to appear again or even worse attack me.

Off in the distance, I could hear my friends carrying on – typical teenage Punk Rock crap.

I stumbled again as I tried to make my way out of the cemetery. I had only stepped into the cemetery by a few feet, yet I'd completely lost my bearings. Acres of the cemetery were in every direction. I wanted to go home and be out of there as quick as possibly.

I called out to my friends. "Where are you?" My voice was panic stricken, filled with fear; there was no hiding it. My friend called back.

"Over here!"

"Over where?" I shouted back. I saw my friend come into view in the distance. I was relieved to see him and to have contact with someone other than the thing that had just made its presence known to me. Blindly, I started walking towards my friend, my eyes fixed on where he was. That was all I cared about. I came to a stop within a few feet of him.

"What the hell are you guys doing?" I asked him, angry at being abandoned.

"Nothing, fooling around I guess..." he replied nonchalantly.

"Fooling around?" I replied. "This is no place to be fooling around! We need to get out of here right now!" I demanded. I had the image of the thing vividly in my mind coupled with the physical illness I was still feeling. "Okay, enough is enough! Get the guys and let's get out of here! Right now!" I insisted.

My friend knew that I was not going to take no for an answer. I had said it with such conviction and command that he didn't even think twice to challenge me. He called out to the others and, one by one, they came and joined us where we stood.

Once we were all together, my friend led us single file out of the cemetery and back to the road where we had parked the car. We walked in silence. I was scared, angry, and upset. I could not shake the image or the feeling. It stuck to me like a waking nightmare, and I was trapped inside.

We piled back into the car. I sat in the driver side back seat. I stared quietly out the window. The guys started chattering again and boasted about their exploits. I said nothing and remained detached from them as I struggled with composure.

A creature, I thought to myself. *How could that be? This stuff doesn't exist, it can't be real!* I continued thinking.

We drove off into the night and soon I was dropped off at my front door. I got out of the car without saying a word. I motioned to them in saying goodnight, and before I turned away, they had sped off down the street. I made my way to the front door, unlocked it, and went inside. It was only minutes before I found myself locked in my room, hiding under the covers of my bed.

What exactly was it that I saw? I cannot say. I can *speculate,* but as time would soon reveal I would come to know the true nature of the energy that I had encountered earlier that night.

High School Years: The Dream

The darkness before me paralyzed my body with the fear. Have I fought in vain? This cannot be my purpose. Low down inside me, the feeling began to grow: terror, hatred, and heavy remorse. I stepped forward, slow and deliberate. Keeping my eyes focused on the blackness, the emptiness, the godlessness. This is what waited for me; I was within its reach. I could smell rotting flesh and decay emanating from this black mass as it heaved and moaned with each huge, deep sigh and hateful breath. It was death incarnate. The un-zoned. The Ancient One. Yog-Sothoth herself. I must continue. One more step closer, it would be over. I need to know the experience of death; I have to see and feel it for myself.

The ground under me began to tremble, threatening to disintegrate. The thing heaved a guttural moan that penetrated all of me, rattling my soul and heart. Its breath was upon me.

Instantly, all feelings dissolved into nothing, my soul hollowed. I stepped forward another step. It moaned and exhaled at me. The stench was gone, but my vision fuzzed. Colors and shapes whirled about me like tribal dancers near a fire. Just beyond the haze, I could still see the shadow of the great beast. For a moment, I felt everything letting go and a euphoric cloud covered me. All was better. Was I winning?

Then, without a hint, the ground convulsed and dropped to an abyss below me. I was pinned to thin air. Immense heat seared my skin and filled the air with the sickening smell. Yet there was no pain in this lucid state.

Then the beast devoured me. I was dissolving into it. I had no care, no want to flee, or to struggle. The light prisms and odd forms came closer and closer. My skin bubbled and began to peel away from the bone; I looked down at my hands and watched the flesh fall. I screamed, not in terror, but pleasure. It was all a backwards game.

Then deep pain attacked. I shrieked and reeled in torment. And I knew a hellish death. I fell back, reaching out, grasping at anything that would stop my fall, but there was nothing.

The nightmare ended and I shot straight up in bed, covered with sweat. It was the fall of 1990. And it was the damn "dream" again, the same dream that had plagued me night after night for weeks. With each night I slept less and less, for as soon as I fell asleep, the dream would begin, come to the same end, bolt me awake, I'd try to sleep – and the whole thing repeated till morning. I knew that this was much more than my subconscious conjuring this terror; it was something greater. That darkness, dread, and lifelessness that surrounded me while awake seemed to stem from this dream.

"How am I supposed to function?" I asked myself out loud. I sobbed into my hands. I stuttered to catch my breath, and with an inhale, the smell that penetrated me in my dreams was in my physical nose. More stress for my teenage life.

I looked up suddenly and saw, in the corner of the room by the door, a dark mass. It was the absence of light more than a solid being. The shape was undefinable. I couldn't tell if it was confined to the corner or if it was infinite. The thing materialized, scared me, and then was gone. Was it ghost or demon?

This being appeared every night along with the nightmare.

The pathetic news was that I had brought this upon myself; this was my burden, my retribution for the things that I had done.

I lay down again and stared at the ceiling. I sniffled and wiped the tears. My breath was captured, and I rolled onto my side and curled into the fetal position. There I would wait for daylight. The alarm clock sat on the bureau at the other side of the room... 3:42 a.m.

Daylight brought school time, another despicable day of wandering hallways in a daze, not caring about anything. I forced myself through the morning ritual and made it to first period with just a few seconds to spare, avoiding another tardy slip.

I hated school and I despised the students except for my few friends. As a junior in a Catholic school, it was a familiar condition, but I rejected the notion of transferring to another institute. However, if my grades continued to flounder, I might not have a choice but to go somewhere else. I knew that the Dean of Studies would welcome that, as he had made it his mission to get me expelled from the school. In his eyes, I was unworthy, but my suspicions were that he feared me. Perhaps this came from my reputation for being a spirit-dabbler.

Many clergy at that school reacted negatively to me. Like Brother George in my freshman year, who had stopped English class dead in its tracks, screamed me out of his class, and, in the hallway, shot spittle in my face as he ranted about my not belonging in his class – all within earshot of the students. I had not done one thing to provoke him. I purposely was not the wave in his ocean, but a dead calm hoping to be left alone. Perhaps some staff member heard this, because within weeks of the outburst he was gone. That was one of many incidents at that school.

This day, I managed to get through with the usual problems, except for study period. *That* was unusual. I had fallen half-asleep and was dreaming, at an open table in front of all of my peers. It was an innocent and simple dream. I dreamt of a cat sitting on my lap and I was simply petting it as it purred and shifted its weight. Unfortunately, I was actually moving my hands and motioning as though I was petting this cat, an embarrassment that my classmates took notice of and began to laugh and joke about. A switch went off in my head; I woke up and caught myself.

"Hey Sarro!" one of the nameless behind me called in a loud whisper.

"What?" I answered as I stared at him, unblinking and unmoving. He had a smirk on his face and his friend sitting next to him looked the same. They stopped smiling and looked away when they noticed the teacher who was monitoring the study period had taken notice of us.

"Mr. Sarro!" he barked. "I suggest you get back to studying or you can join me again at 3 p.m. for detention!" I motioned in submission and buried my head in my geometry book, pretending to study. The class got quiet.

Geometry to me was useless shapes on a page: triangles, squares, parallelograms. But I found myself continuously drawing over the shapes, then one shape in particular, making the same symbol over and over again in as many different ways as I could. It was the pentagram, a five-pointed star, the mixture of two triangles encapsulated within a circle.

This symbol haunted me. I obsessed over it and drew it whenever compelled. It was on the cover of every textbook, making them worthless for resale by the school.

I got home from school, late as usual, since I had detention everyday as part of my academic probation. The threat of detention from my teachers was pointless.

I went straight to my room, closed the door, dropped my book bag on my desk chair, turned to the bed, and fell face down.

It was still daylight. The days were getting shorter now as fall rolled into winter. I had to steal any moment I could to sleep before sundown, because, like clockwork, the nightmare would return. I fell asleep. My body became paralyzed. I felt the dread. *Oh, no, here it comes.*

"Mark." I heard a woman's voice call out to me. "Mark," it said louder. "Mark, its dinner time!" Mom was calling.

I woke suddenly; it was dark and just past 6 p.m. I had beaten the dream. I wasn't hungry, but forced myself to eat something so that I wouldn't attract any attention from my family. I did my best to hide all paranormal issues from them. But school was something else. They were fully aware of my failing grades and lack of interest in making them better.

The tormenting struggle with the spirit realm I handled alone, except for my good friends, Bill and Dave. They had no choice since they were my paranormal "partners."

I finished dinner, did the dishes, and went to my room to try and do the homework that I had ignored from last week. I never did my homework; I never studied for tests; I simply couldn't do it. I was too distracted by the ethereal.

I sat at my desk with my English book open. The clock read 8:15 p.m. I was tired and fading; my eyes grew heavier and heavier as the words on the page blurred. I put my head down, but only for a moment, I thought.

I stood alone in the darkness. It was so dark that I could not gauge the size of the room or any sense of direction or bearing. The floor trembled beneath me and the movement was so strong that I lost my balance and fell. I felt around me and the surface was cold and smooth – too hard for natural earth, not stone either, but artificial. I was definitely in a room and not outside.

In that moment, something slithered across my hand; I pulled back, startled and uncertain. Then something brushed behind me as it passed. I turned and reached out, trying to push it away, but nothing was there. I rose to my feet and turned back again in the other direction. The ground rumbled again and I heard the heavy breathing and gurgling of something lurking in the darkness before me. Stinking breath surrounded me and filled my senses with decay, rotting, death. It consumed me and was heavy. The ground moved again and I felt this thing coming closer to me. The demon of my dreams was at me again. Its purpose was to corrupt, to destroy, and turn anyone who came within its presence mad with hysteria. The flashes of color began to flicker before me; unrecognizable shapes intermingling with each other; defying gravity and logic. Another sodden breath and moan said the beast had drawn closer.

Suddenly, I gained awareness. I was dreaming. It needed to end, but I was powerless to do anything about it, and felt more frightened and helpless. The beast lured me closer. I stepped forward. The flashes of color leaped about me; fire began to flash. I was weaker, and fully aware of the horror. The acrid smell of burning flesh began to fill my nostrils. It was my flesh burning. The pain was beyond words, but I remained still.

Another step forward. The beast grabbed me.

Out of the darkness now, its shape and size was apparent. It looked down, hovering above me. Drool fell from its gaping mouth onto my arm and burned like acid. I closed my eyes and began to sway. I leaned my head back and laughed the laugh of madness, insanity, and chaos.

There was a pressure on my right shoulder, and something softly spoke my name. I awoke and jumped up from my desk to find my mother standing beside me with a look of curiosity and worry.

"Mark, are you alright?" she asked.

"Umm, yeah, I think so..." I said as I tried to play down the terror that was running through me.

"You were asleep and wouldn't wake up," she said.

"I'm okay. Homework got me again," I said as I smirked and motioned to my English book sitting open on my desk.

"If you're so tired, then you should go to bed," she stated as she turned and left my room, closing the door behind her. I looked back at the clock on my desk again. 10:30 p.m. I'd lost over two hours? I felt as though I had only just fallen asleep. The exhaustion was so great that my limbs were heavy and ached. I flopped in the chair and looked about the room. It was dark except for the floor lamp next to my desk with its low wattage bulb.

I turned towards the corner of my room. Something had drawn my attention. It was darker than it should have been, considering that there was some light in the room. It was unnaturally dark, yet there was nothing noticeable enough to tell if something was actually there or not. I sat and watched. The corner grew darker as it seemed that all light was being sucked away into a vacuum. Something was forming. It slowly began to fill the corner. It went from the floor to ceiling. Its mass was still undefined, save for the darkness. My mind recoiled in horror as I sat motionless watching it. It became more and more solid and still had no definable features or shape; it was simply a black mass filling up the corner of the room. I leapt from my chair, not once taking my eyes off of it. I moved myself onto the bed and backed against the wall for a good look. I wasn't sure it was real. Night after night, as I awoke from the nightmare, it seemed that there was something in the room, but it had never come into view as it was now and never when I was completely awake.

This time it had waited until I was awake before it materialized.

And then it was gone.

The Truth is Told: The Lies Revealed

Necronomicon, as anyone with a search engine can learn, is a work of fiction. This information was not so readily available twenty years ago. It took me months of research and investigating to get to the bottom of the mystery that surrounded this dark text.

Its origination started with its mention in several short stories by H.P. Lovecraft. The book does reference actual historical deities, texts, vernacular, and places that go far back into the ancient Sumerian civilization, but the written language used in this book, that was supposed to be Sumerian, was a mix of gibberish and actual words and phrases found in the ancient tablets from that time. The version that made itself present in my life was the one that went to paperback in 1980 and is still available on Simon Press. It has sold over 800,000 copies worldwide.

I would not make the discovery about the book until my senior year in high school, when I wrote a final term paper for my English class. I chose the subject; the *Necronomicon* and H.P. Lovecraft's ties to the work.

Initially, I thought that the book came before H.P. Lovecraft's stories, and believed that *his* work was a direct result of the inspiration from ancient text. I learned it was the other way around.

This was a valuable lesson in matters of researching and investigating the paranormal. The disturbing question that immediately arose within me was: "If these things were not real, then what was it that I encountered after I started reading the book?" The answer would come years later.

Over time, I shed the illusions of this book and the effects that it had on my psyche and emotional state. Although the creatures, demons, and gods in this book were fictionalizations, I *did* encounter some form of dark intelligence that preyed on my weaknesses, and exploited beliefs that grew from the book. My subconscious projected images from the book back onto the dark intelligence. It is the ultimate manipulator, agent of deceit, and portrayer of lies.

This definition would apply to the Christian Devil, but my experience says that things of this nature transcend far beyond any religious influence. These things *do exist* and are a part of our own metaphysical and spiritual history. I have worked many cases over the years since these times where I have encountered energies and darker forces. The idea of a demon or devil is yet another machination produced by the doctrinal teachings of the religions of the world. We must release those preconceived notions in order to understand the darkness.

As I look back on the experiences that I gained from age eleven to age seventeen, I see how vulnerable I was to negative energy. It fed upon all the things that I willingly gave to it. Dangerous, this was, and had life-altering effects on me and others.

Now I recognize the signs when energy like this is present in someone's home or is attached to an individual. Because of this, I'm often able to provide an individual or family the tools and resources to combat these things on their own. My direct experiences with dark things help me to help others come to terms with these issues. Best of all, with some common sense, others can avoid these paranormal problems altogether.

Did this energy seek me out or did I indirectly seek it? Once here, it stayed for quite some time. When I am chatting with peers, or giving lectures and seminars, I always say that, "once you are on the radar of these types of negative things, you are always on it. It sees you and is aware of you as much as you can see or be aware of it!"

Pike Creek Valley, New Castle County

"SATAN HOUSE"

Satan House, Witch's House, Devil House – there is something to be said about this urban legend. Satan House was a story I first heard as a teenager.

The building sits back off the road atop a hill in a deep, dark, wooded area of the Pike Creek Valley near the Pennsylvania border. I would have dismissed the story as folklore if the following tale wasn't told first-hand by a friend and fellow musician who grew up in the area, and who visited the property.

It was a late Saturday night when we decided to see Satan House for ourselves. I didn't believe the stories, but I've had my share of weird experiences. I was intrigued. We turned off the main highway onto a back road. Slowly we made our way down this road. It became narrower and narrower. I would find out later that we were drawing closer to the house.

There was a creek to our left, and all of the trees that grew along the creek bed were aimed out across the water. The trees gave the appearance of trying to escape the house, like hands reaching for help. All of a sudden, a pair of headlights appeared behind us. At first, the lights were at least 100 yards back, but quickly they made up the distance and soon were on top of us.

We panicked and didn't know what to do. Our driver suddenly pulled off into a driveway on the right. This was a mistake. The car skidded to a stop behind us and blocked us in the driveway. I turned in my seat and saw the vehicle was a black SUV. I couldn't tell the make and model. The lights must have been on high beams because they reached over the trunk of our car and blinded us. It was a horror-movie come true.

Then, one by one the doors of the SUV opened and out stepped these men; they all were at least six-foot- five-inches, or taller, broad shouldered, and all had long hair that practically went down to their waists. They hunched forward, almost slouching as they stood there silently.

Slowly, their driver lumbered to our driver's window. He knocked on the window with his closed fist. My friend reluctantly rolled down his window. "You don't belong here. You must leave now," the man said in a low gruff voice, as he motioned with his hand for us to get off the property.

None of us except our driver got a good look at him. My friend was speechless but for one muttered word: "grotesque." His body shook as he rolled the window up.

The man quickly turned and went back to the SUV. I watched as all four men climbed back into the truck at exactly the same time. The truck pulled back violently and swung around onto the road facing in the direction that we were to go. My friend backed the car down the driveway and out onto the road. We drove off slow and steady. The SUV followed us as we made our way down the road and eventually came to the common road. We turned right onto the main road, and the SUV stopped at the intersection and waited for us to drive off. I looked back to see what the truck would do and it just sat there as we drove. Once we got a little further away, the truck pulled out onto the main road, swung violently into a U-turn, and headed back from where they came.

We were shook to our core, but our driver seemed more affected. He was the only one to face the strange men. To this day, I can hear my friend mutter "grotesque" to describe the face of the man that he saw.

This account was one of sincerity and such conviction that I had to believe her.

Now the curiosity was peaked in *me*. I had to find the house and see it for myself. Would the mysterious black SUV pursue us and drive us off the land? Would the giants that appeared outside the SUV be there as well? From that moment on, I had openly discussed it with my friend and her boyfriend, who happened to be one of my band mates at the time.

We pondered night after night about the house and wondered aloud as to the possibilities of what the house was, who the inhabitants were, and why they were doing such things. One of the scenarios that we spun was that it was a front for a drug house or meth lab and we would go in via SWAT style and raid the house and see what was really going on. Of course, this was a fantasy; neither one of us was equipped to even consider doing such a thing, not to mention how very illegal the act of performing a "raid" on the house would have been.

Still, I was determined to see the house for myself. I began hearing chatter from different circles of friends and acquaintances as far as the lore and legend of the Satan House.

There was a nickname going around for the people in the house that they were "Zoobies." A Zoobie was the supposed offspring of incestuous family bloodlines from a prominent family from Delaware. Another speculation about the house and its occupants were that they were a satanic coven who had dwelled in the house for many years and practiced all sorts of black magic and satanic rites. For some reason, though, the idea of either of these scenarios did not scare me off. I still had to go and see for myself what this house was about.

A Road Trip

The night of the quest to find the house was unplanned. Despite the weeks of talk and speculation about the house and how we would go about visiting the place, we did not plan for it. To put it into perspective, I was only nineteen at the time. I was staying with my sister and her husband and was a couch dweller of sorts. Her husband was kind enough to let me use his van from time to time as needed for general transportation or for band use during shows. The van was an old brown cargo van, rusted out in spots and quirky about how it drove. It took a certain finesse to get the van to actually move forward. One of the very first times I tried to use the van, it would stall out every few feet and sputter and cough as it lurched to a stop.

So, on this particular night, I had been hanging with Wayne, the guitarist of my current band, along with Charlie, Chris, Niles, Freddy Dynamite, and a few others (whose names now elude me). At some point in the night, discussion of the house began and a plan leapt into action.

"Let's go to Satan House," Wayne exclaimed.

"Damn straight!" I replied with excitement.

One of the other guys in the group that night chimed up that he knew exactly where it was. So, we piled into the old brown Chevy van and off into the night we drove. It approached 1 a.m. before we had even decided to start this adventure.

Turn by turn, my navigator got us into the general area of the house; we then turned onto the infamous road where the house stood. It was dark. Very dark. The headlights were consumed by the blackness around us. The woods were dense and surrounded us on all sides; off to the left, through the trees, you could barely see the creek that lurked in the darkness. The road was narrow, and now I was experiencing it firsthand from behind the wheel; driving a quirky old van that could stall, sputter, and decide to take a break at any moment.

The anxiety was growing inside me, but the excitement was enough to keep it at bay. Besides, I had eight guys in the van with me; what's the worst that could happen? The closer we got to the house, the more peculiar the trees began to look. As my friend told me her story, the memories of her events were now playing before my eyes. The trees were growing out away from the road like hands grasping to hold the night sky.

The road twisted and turned alongside the creek and was at times so narrow that there would be no way for opposing traffic to get by despite the fact that it was a two-way road. I slowed the vehicle down to a crawl pace. We were getting closer and I wanted to be sure not to miss it. I had to see it. I was also one for adding a dramatic effect and admittedly a bit reckless. I had decided to turn off the headlights.

The van slowly crawled through the void of the night; darkness consuming and swallowing us whole as we blended into the landscape. An eerie silence consumed the van and everyone inside. Before there was idle chatter and conversation going on amongst the group, but now all was quiet as we inched closer and closer to the house. Wayne was on lookout for the house and the mysterious black SUV that we expected to pull out and run us off at any moment.

"There it is!" Wayne called out as he pointed through the window of the van and up the hill to the right. A long narrow driveway that curved and twisted uphill led directly to the house. It was dark, not a light came from within, yet it stood out enough that, even in the total darkness of the woods, we were able to see it.

I brought the van to a complete stop as we sat in the road at the bottom of the driveway. The house perched atop the hill looked down upon us like a sentinel keeping watch on a castle wall. We sat there quietly, the van purring with the occasional hiccup as the engine struggled to keep running.

I stared intently at the house, my mind going in a million directions as to what lay behind its doors... *Who lives there?* I asked myself. *What are they doing here?* I thought. All these questions and curiosities, yet I lacked the courage to turn and drive up the driveway or to get out of the van to take a closer look. I was completely happy with staying within the security of the van alongside my eight companions.

There was still no sign of the black SUV.

Maybe they have the night off? I thought to myself. Wayne then turned and looked at me with that devilish smile that he often wore, and wore too well. He didn't have to say a word; I knew what he was thinking, but there was no way I was going up there.

"No," I quietly and sternly spoke to him. He quickly accepted and understood that there would be no convincing or coercing me into getting out of the van and making our way through the woods up to the house.

I kept a keen eye in the rearview and side mirrors. I was waiting for the headlights to come on out of nowhere as the legends foretold. Still nothing.

"Okay, I think it's time to go!" I said aloud to the group. I put the van into drive and began to crawl forward again. I waited until we were securely past the house (or as secure as we were going to be) before I turned the headlights back on. We continued moving down the road and eventually came to the main road. It was the same road where my friend had been followed by the black SUV. I was disappointed and relieved at the same time, as far as the appearance of the SUV was concerned. I really did not have the energy to confront and deal with the result of the SUV chasing us down.

We turned right onto the main road and made our way back out of the area and back into safety. The night was drawing to a close; one by one, I dropped my friends off and eventually ended up home at about a 3:45 a.m.

I came into the house, dropped the keys on the counter, and crashed out on the couch. My mind was still abuzz with the night's adventure, even though nothing had happened. I searched my mind and all the possibilities of what lay behind the doors of the house. "Who lived there?" "Where was the black SUV?" "What things took place in that house?" All these questions and more crept through my mind. How long was "Satan House" there? Where did the urban legend get started? How long has it been referred to as "Satan House?"

In conclusion, I cannot speak to how this story became urban legend. Safe to say, that I had heard the stories from various people starting in high school, and since then, the lore of the house has been mentioned on various websites and other publications. At the point where I am now in my life, I can honestly say that it wasn't, or isn't, worth the risk to search out the house and see it again. I was lucky not to have a traumatic experience or confrontation, but at least I can say I've been to "Satan House."

Sussex County – A little History

During its pre-colonial to present-day existence, Sussex County has seen the same influx of western European discoverers as the rest of the state. Those who stayed, generally, became farmers, tapping into local resources and staking claims into regional property on which to build new lives. While being the largest of the three state counties, Sussex is historically the least populated. However, that has never stopped the good people of Sussex from winning their share of the state limelight. As far back as 1763, Deep Creek Iron Forge was constructed, jump starting iron work in the county.

In 1791, plans were plotted out to build Georgetown and make it the new county seat, relieving the town of Lewes of the job and setting the seat in a more central location in the county. Perhaps this was a premonition since, during the War of 1812, the British bombarded the sea town of Lewes.

The first railroad reached Delmar in 1859. For the first time, local farmers could transport their produce out of state to the larger communities of Philadelphia and Baltimore, greatly increasing revenues.

An odd clerical error created another boon for Sussex County in 1923, when Cecile Steele of Ocean View ordered fifty baby chicks for her egg business, but received 500 by mistake. This foul-up fueled the modern broiler trade and made Sussex County both the birthplace and the number one producer of chickens in the United States. Lovely Sussex County is now home to seaside resorts, industry, and agriculture.

CHASING DOWN THE LEGEND OF THE WITCHES TREE

On the afternoon of Halloween 2011, my co-author Gerry and I embarked on a day trip to gather stories and information related to some reportedly haunted sites and urban legends. We had driven down to Cape Henlopen and purchased a camp site as our base of operations for the day and night. The other locations that we had to investigate were further south.

We set out to track down and find the "Witches Tree" that was reported to be in Selbyville, Delaware. The little town was about thirty minutes further south from Cape Henlopen.

When we arrived, we didn't know it! The town was unassuming and sat along a main road with only a couple of traffic lights. As we drove onto the town's main road, we realized the reports of the Witches Tree only brought us to the general area and not an exact location. We were going to have to start asking around to see if anyone knew where this tree was located.

This is where things can get interesting; two strangers roll into town on the afternoon of Halloween and start asking questions about a Witches Tree. Yes, priceless.

I figured the best place to ask would be at a convenience store. If they look at you crazy and ask you to leave, it's no big deal! Unfortunately, there were no convenience stores in town, or at least that we saw. On our left, as we drove further, came the town public library. The local library can be the source to tap into all things specific to a town.

The car was parked and we strode toward the front door. As we approached, there were several folks standing out front on the sidewalk talking; they noticed us, but did not think much of it as we looked like two unassuming guys who were strangers in their town. One of them noticed that we were headed towards the library door when they spoke up.

"Sorry, the library's closed today. We're decorating for Halloween."

We thanked them for the information and asked about the Witches Tree. They were receptive to our inquiry and several of them remarked that they had heard of it, but it wasn't in Selbyville. They said that the tree was in Frankford, Delaware, which was just a few miles north of Selbyville. The four locals proceeded to tell us about the library and how it was haunted by the ghost of Mr. Townsend, who lived there when it was his private residence. He later willed the property to the town for a library. Since the building was closed, we were unable to check it out further.

The people were very kind and invited us to come back for the evening's event. But our next stop would be Frankford. Gerry and I set off again for the Witches Tree which now, supposedly, grew in Frankford. The town was only a few miles up the road, and was even smaller than Selbyville. We actually drove through it, back and forth a couple of times before we realized that we were, in fact, inside the town itself. We searched for any public building where we might be able to stop and ask for information, but initially we could not locate one.

I then spotted a little antique store off to the right. It was the only public place that seemed open. We pulled up alongside the store and someone came out to greet us before we even got out of the car. Gerry decided that he would get out and ask and that I would stay in the car. He approached the woman standing on the front porch of her store and began to ask her about the tree that we were "desperate" to find. I rolled down my window so that I could hear. Sometimes, you never know which way it may go. I learned the hard way while writing *Ghosts of West Chester* (Pennsylvania) that, occasionally, you will get a few doors closed in your face!

But the woman was very kind and pointed Gerry in the direction of the local historian. He happened to live across the street from where we were, but he had taken his granddaughter to a baseball game and would not be back for a few hours. Unfortunately, we did not have that much time on our hands, as we wanted to get back to the base camp at Cape Henlopen before nightfall. It was already late in the afternoon, so we knew that our time was running out.

The woman also suggested that we go to the local library to see if anyone there had any information. We showed our gratitude and sped off to the Frankford Public Library. It was a long ride, perhaps seven seconds. The library was around the corner, one block away. Upon entering, we were greeted by a young woman working behind the counter. Being in the spirit of Halloween, she was dressed from head to toe as a witch, and was complete with a hat and broom (which was leaning up against the counter behind her as she helped several other gentlemen check out books from the library).

I approached the counter and asked her politely if she had heard about the "Witches Tree" and if she knew where it might be.

"I have no idea," she answered after a moment's thought.

Two middle-aged men standing near the counter had heard the exchange. I am sure they were wondering, "Was this guy for real?" as the look on their faces clearly implied.

"Have you guys heard of the Witches Tree and would you know where it is?" I asked the men. They kept their original facial expressions and simply shook their heads.

The young witch behind the counter then spoke up and said that we should ask the librarian who runs the children's library. "Let me check and see if she is available," she said politely and then picked up the phone to ring her extension.

Keep in mind that this library was the size of a small house. It would have been just as effective if she had called out since the lady stood about twenty feet away.

The witch told us that the librarian would talk to us and pointed us in her direction. Gerry and I took about ten steps to the other end of the counter, around the corner and there she was. The librarian had the stoic look of someone who'd worked there a long time. She gave us a warm greeting.

"Have you heard of the Witches Tree, and do you happen to know where we can find it?" Like the other librarian, she paused for a moment.

"I have never heard of such a thing, and I have been living here for thirty years."

That was enough for me. When someone tells you that they've never heard of something that supposedly takes place in their town, when the town is as small as this one was, then you know that, more than likely, the place you are looking for doesn't exist!

The lady sensed our looming defeat.

"Let me call someone," she said. "He is the local historian, and if anyone was to know if such a thing existed he would."

We followed her around back to the front counter where the witch was still working her magic on the mystical book checkout by the same two gentlemen who were standing there a moment ago, still amused by the exchange going on between Gerry, the librarian, and myself. I informed the librarian that we already knew the historian was at his granddaughter's baseball game. She called him anyway and left a message with our cell number, to call *us* if he knew anything about the Witches Tree.

We thanked both the librarian and the witch as well and bid farewell to the pair of guys hanging out, listening to our inquiry. At that point, Gerry and I decided that it was time to throw in the towel and head back to Cape Henlopen. This had been the last stop on our day's journey, and we wanted to be sure to get back to the camp site with plenty of time to take advantage of the daylight so that we could prepare for the evening's investigation.

Needless to say, I never heard back from the librarian or the historian. It was apparent that the urban legend of the Witches Tree was in fact just that, and had no basis of fact.

BUZZZZZZ – survey says: no Witches Tree.

In an age of technology, with vast amounts of information at our fingertips, only a click away from search engines that bring instant data, there is also a ton of false information and claims that simply are not true. It is important to dig beyond the surface when these claims are reported. Unfortunately, there are those who like to make up stories and promote them as facts. It's a cautionary tale on the importance of being earnest, and not Earnest from *Earnest goes to Jail*. Know what I mean, *Vern*?

CYPRESS SWAMP, SUSSEX COUNTY

The road that cuts directly through Cypress swamp is a pleasant one to drive during the day; a simple two-lane road that has a dense canopy of trees as well as thick underbrush mixed within the trees. We set upon the road on a mild Halloween afternoon and made our way to one end of the swamp and back. It's actually difficult to see the swamp through the trees, but Gerry and I knew it was there. The urban legend involving this road is that, while driving along late at night, you can hear disembodied voices coming from the woods, chanting and speaking in weird tongues. There was no time to study the area. But I felt obliged to at least visit the site as I did receive an anonymous story about an experience that happened along the road.

Voices in the Night

We were driving along Cypress Swamp Road late one summer night. It was about 2:00 a.m. We were headed back from a friend's place. We live nearby and often use this road as a shortcut. We had the windows down and were driving slow. The road at night is very dark with all the trees and such and I didn't want to run the risk of hitting a deer... We

The road through the swamp. In the story, the truck was parked off to the left where the chanting voices were heard calling out into the night.

got about halfway into the swamp when we started hearing voices. They sounded like a group of men, chanting something, but we couldn't understand what it was. I looked at my girlfriend and asked her if she was hearing what I was hearing and she looked at me wide-eyed, so I knew she heard it. We slowed the truck down to a crawl. There was no one behind us, so I didn't have to worry about any traffic or anything. As we slowed down, the voices got louder. I'm not sure if we were driving *towards* them or what, but they were definitely louder. I decided to stop the truck off to the side of the road and turn out the lights. We sat there for a few minutes while we listened and couldn't believe what we were hearing! My girl got really upset and said we should leave immediately. I thought it was cool, but felt like if I didn't do what she said, I wasn't gonna get any that night! I'm just bein' honest! So, we took off in a hurry and got out of there! Ever since then she doesn't let me drive down that road if it's late at night. It freaks her out too much, so now we gotta go the long way!"

~Anonymous

I had a similar experience in Newark when I was a teenager. I wonder if what they heard *wasn't spirits*, but an occult group. He didn't describe what the chanting was, so it is difficult to speculate what the voices might have been saying. Either way, I understand how it may make one upset or uncomfortable.

Southern Delaware
Other Quick Haunts

Woonsocket

MOUNT SAINT CHARLES ACADEMY

The spirit of a brother who was a former administrator for the school is reported to roam the fourth floor, looking for revenge. The story goes that some students decided to stick pencils in his eyes at his funeral and now, in the afterlife, he wants to get back at any unsuspecting student he can!

Frankford

GRAVEYARD

Supposedly, if you go to the brick wall at the back of the graveyard and knock three times (Oh no!) a half cat/half man (were-panther?) will come out and start to give you car trouble; your car won't start and he will continue to walk around the graveyard and wait for you!

Fredrica

HIGHWAY 12 WEST

There are reports of a dog with red glowing eyes being seen on this highway. The urban legend reports include a murder where the murderer fed his victim to his dog.

Seaford

AIRPORT ROAD

The ghost of a weeping Valentine's Day bride is said to be seen walking along the road, and the ghost of a Confederate soldier is seen as well.

Seaford

MAGGIE'S BRIDGE

Apparently, the spirit of "Maggie" is seen walking down by the creek and on the bridge. Cars will malfunction and have issues on the bridge.

A Generation Says Farewell

Time to Say Goodbye

My Grandfather, Lawrence P. Bensinger, was a great man. I only got to have him for a short time in my life, but the impression he made on me will stay with me until my end of days. He passed away in June of 1988.

During the interview I conducted with my grandmother about the family, we also talked about Grandpop, too. My mother and grandmother, along with other members of the family, were there at the final moments of his life. He had fought a hard battle with cancer and did his best to hang in there for all of us, but like the eventuality for all of us, his time to move on had come.

A WELCOMING TO ANEW...

On the day that he died, in those final moments, he became extremely lucid. Grandmother was by his side. He looked at her and drew her in close saying: "Without you there would be nothing; because of you, we had everything." My grandmother spoke in a quiet, soft voice as she told me this, then said with the same tone *to me* "When he said that, I knew the time had come."

My mother recalled an experience that she witnessed in the moments just before Grandpop passed and the moment's right after.

> I was standing by the window when he passed. I looked out the window and I saw three white doves flying towards the hospital window. They had passed by above the window and out of view; a few moments later Dad passed. Then I looked out and saw the three doves flying away from the hospital and a fourth dove that was trying to catch up and join the other two. This happened right after he had died.

You cannot deny the spiritual significance of this kind of experience; to witness the moment of one's transformation from this life to the next, and physically see a sign of the spirit moving on from the physical to the next world. This is something truly amazing and blessed.

A WARM EMBRACE

In the years after his passing, there have been more than several instances where his presence was felt and experienced by my mother, my grandmother, and me, as well as other members of my family. My grandmother recounted several experiences that she had with my grandfather after he had passed.

On several occasions my grandmother would come into the den where my grandfather would sit in his favorite chair and read. He sat in that chair the same way he did in life. It would be a brief encounter, but one that repeated itself several times over the years. As the time grew longer since his passing, it became less and less frequent.

My grandmother also recalled several times when my grandfather would visit her in a dream. They often would sit at a table and look at each other. Without saying a word, they would communicate by a look. Oftentimes, he was there simply to make his presence known and to offer comfort to my grandmother when she needed him most. On one of his dream visits, she woke up with the feeling that he had climbed into bed and "spooned" with her. She remembers that the feeling was as though he *was* there, but quickly the feeling faded and his presence was gone.

My grandfather has come to me on more than one occasion to visit in *my* dreams. He never spoke a word, but he never had to. There was a mutual understanding that neither of us should be there. But we knew for that brief moment when our two worlds merged that it was good. He had a way of looking at you. Without any words, you knew and understood exactly what he was saying. Every time that he has ever come to visit me in my dreams, it has been in that same way. No words spoken, but yet the message was clear.

There was an instance when he had come to visit me while I was living in the house in West Chester, Pennsylvania. I was still together with my wife at the time; but this time, he wasn't in my dreams, but standing over on my side of the bed. Kat, my wife then, woke to see him standing there, watching after me. He was wearing a red, plaid, flannel shirt. He did not acknowledge Kat, but remained quiet and looked on as I slept. I still have several of his shirts, and more specifically, a red plaid one that was eerily similar to the one he was wearing when seen by my ex. I wrote about that story in detail in my first book *Ghosts of West Chester* (available through Schiffer Books, Amazon or Barnes and Noble).

The most recent story of a visitation from my grandfather to a family member comes from my sister. This experience happened only a week before I had to turn in the manuscript for this book (November 2011). My sister recently bought a home in Smyrna, Delaware, and since moving into the house, she has welcomed two new additions to her household – both of them dogs. One of her newest dogs is a Beagle mix. He was standing in the kitchen, and all of a sudden started barking and wagging his tail, as if someone was standing directly in front of him. My sister witnessed the activity as it went on for several minutes and clearly there was no one there. As soon as the moment passed, she immediately had thoughts of Grandpop. We were chatting online when she told me the story and I had asked her several questions about what had taken place. She remarked about how uncanny it was that immediately she thought of Grandpop and instinctively knew that it was he who had just "visited" her. Grandpop was always partial to Beagles and had them as pets for many years. It seems as though, for that fleeting moment, he was there to say hello to my sister's dog.

I PUT YOUR NAME IN THE BIBLE

My grandmother's spirituality is a testament to the innate abilities that exist in my mother's side of the family. She is a devout Christian and strongly believes in the power of prayer and positive affirmations. As part of my interview with her, she talked about her spirituality and faith.

Anytime that I find out that something is wrong and isn't going well for somebody, I go to the Bible on my nightstand and put their name on a piece of paper and put it in the Bible. I think about them and their needs and I ask Jesus to provide them with their needs. I praise Him and pray for them. "I ask and I shall receive." That's my faith. I believe that and I have since I was a little girl. I've used the same Bible all my life."

She has had a picture of the Blessed Mother since she was a little girl. The picture survived a fire and still has the burnt edges. Her spirituality and belief in the power of prayer has had a positive impact on all of those in the family who have ever had a hard time in their life. I know, because I have been a direct recipient of her prayers and affirmations. Through the course of my life, she has put my name in her Bible several times when I needed it most.

Today, my grandmother is 94 years old. She is the oldest of twelve siblings who lived until adulthood, 7 of which are still alive. She has 4 children, 15 grandchildren, 21 great grandchildren and 3 great-great grandchildren. The history of my grandparents and great grandparents are an integral part of the paranormal history of my family. I could not reasonably tell one history without sharing the history of the other.

I thank God for all the good things that happened in my life... I'm proud that I have such a great family. I know I miss my husband, but he'd be very proud of all of them.

~Mary Bensinger
Mother, Grandmother, Great-grandmother and
Great-great-grandmother.

The Cape Henlopen Memoirs

Observation Tower 7 is open to the
public and sits just across the road
from the entrance to Fort Miles.

During World War II, Fort Miles was assembled just south of Lewes, Delaware, as part of the east coast defense network. It would be the first line of defense in keeping Nazi forces from reaching the shipping center in Wilmington and the naval shipbuilding yard in Philadelphia, Pennsylvania. Fort Miles's best claim was that it accepted the surrender of Nazi U-boat, U-858. The German captain and crew sailed into Cape Henlopen on May 14, 1945, and handed the submarine to Fort Miles authorities. Germany had already surrendered on May 7, 1945. Today, the fort is part of Cape Henlopen State Park.

Date: Monday, September 19 and Monday, October 31, 2011
Participants: Mark, Gerry, and Norma Orteza, founder of Past Intel, a paranormal research group based out of Downingtown, Pennsylvania, (http://www.youtube.com/pastintel)

What follows is a transcription of *some* of the audio recordings taken at an investigations conducted at Fort Miles. While the two sessions lasted about five hours over the two days, most of the time was spent doing EVPs. This is a slow process since a pause must follow each question to give a spirit time to answer, and not until the recordings are played back through a computer program hours, days, or weeks later, do you find any answers. The Frank's Box, commonly called the Ghost Box, is a radio scanning device and gives real time responses from...whomever. There is one segment here from EVP, included only for its historic content. The rest of the transcripts are from the Ghost Box.

The view from atop Observation Tower 7, off in the distance another tower peers above the trees.

The entrance road to Fort Miles.

The Old Barracks

First, we went to the old barracks in the fort. They were constructed of a concrete floor; white, cement block walls; green, wooden windows and gray, heavy wooden doors; and open-gabled, unfinished wooden ceilings. The fort buildings and guns were in a moderately good state of preservation.

Mark: "Session four, in building T606. We will attempt communication using the Ghost Box sweep radio."

Each session lasted about twenty minutes. There were no actual beds in any of the buildings, however there were marks left on the floor from dividing walls and bunk beds that had been removed.

Norma: "Who slept at this bunk right here, during the U-boat surrender at Ft. Miles?"

Ghost Box: "Fields."

Mark: "Were you a private?"

Ghost Box: "Correct."

Mark: "Private Fields, how long did you live in this barrack?"

Ghost Box: "Get off this place."

Spirits often tell investigators to leave. Reason: perhaps they are uncomfortable with us, or feel we are intruding.

Mark: "Private Fields, we need a direct answer. How long were you stationed here?"

Ghost Box: "Two months."

Mark: "Are there any other privates here? If so, please state your last name."

The Ghost Box began to chatter.

Norma: (to the crew) "They're saying quite a bit, but I can't make it out." (To the spirits) "What is the name of this building we are in?"

Ghost Box: "Barracks."

Mark: "Thanks for communicating with us. Is there anything else you'd like to tell us?"

Ghost Box: "Every country."

This odd comment was not addressed since time was running short.

Mark: "Private Fields and the other men who served here, thank you for talking with us." This is the end of session four.

The Beach

Next, we moved down to the beach. Our location on the beach was about twenty yards north of the south side sixteen-inch gun emplacement. This massive armament was encased in concrete that was set in a hill at the rear of the dunes. It was not visible from the beach.

Mark had a map from *National Geographic* that showed the names of ships and the dates they sunk in the surrounding waters between Prime Hook Beach and Dewey Beach in the south. That is a distance of only about seventeen miles. The map listed over seventy-five ships lost. The hauntings reported had been about seeing ghost ships on the ocean, spirits walking the beach, and voices heard when there was no one around. It was our hope to experience and record one or more of these phenomena. This is the EVP segment.

Mark: "We are on the shore of Cape Henlopen State Park. It is 3:38 p.m. We are directly in front of Fort Miles, on the beach. The high tide was at 1:44 p.m. with a wave height of 4.4 feet, and the next low tide is at 8:10 p.m. with a wave height expected to be 1.1 feet. We are in close proximity of the following shipwrecks:"

Ship Name	Date Sunk
Harry K. Fooks	9/10/1941
Hesper	4/30/1919
Delaware	10/14/1746
Happy Return	9/1747
Sarah W. Lawrence	2/10/1909
Morris	4/11/1777
William	1855
J.W. Folsom	1855
Medway	10/25/1872
L. J. Westway	12/30/1886
Two unidentified ships	3/16/1760 & 9/1785

Mark: "Also, this is the location where ghost ships have been seen out in the water. The *National Geographic's* map does not give the distance the ships were from the shore when they sank. We will cross-reference with longitude and latitude readings to hopefully pinpoint the mileage from the shore if we see a ghost ship. On the map, many of the ships appear to have crashed on the beach. There have also been reports of ghost figures on the beach walking towards the lighthouse which is four to five miles north from here. We will begin session number five here on the beach in hopes of communicating with any lost souls. It is now 3:41 p.m. The temperature is 67.7 degrees F. EMF base line is 0.0."

The investigators decide which ship's crew to address. They pick the *Sarah W. Lawrence.*

Mark: "Crew members of the *Sarah W. Lawrence*, from 1909, we know that you met your demise here. If any of you are trapped here, this is your chance to come forward and communicate. Come to us on this beach and tell us your story. If there are any officers from the ship, please tell us your name and rank. If there are any passengers who are on shore, please tell us your names."

After a pause to record any answers that might be captured by the EVP device, Mark addressed the crew of a second ship.

Mark: "Crew members and passengers of the ship *Happy Return*, we know that you came ashore in September of 1747, right off of Cape Henlopen. Any crew members who may have come ashore, please tell us your name and rank, or position on the ship."

Session five was ended.

The Ghost Box was turned on and held near the recorder.

Norma: "Temperature is 69.4 degrees."

Mark: "This is session number six. We will continue with our questions."

Norma: "Who's been walking up and down the shoreline?"

Gerry: "What was the name of your ship that sank?"

Ghost Box: "Can't swim."

Norma: "What was the name of your ship?"

Ghost Box: "Who is this?"

Norma: "This is Norma."

Gerry: "What town are you trying to reach?"

Norma: "How many crew members were on your ship?"

Ghost Box: "Twenty-six."

Norma: "What was the name of your ship?"

The Ghost Box's response sounded like U...something, but the full response was not clearly understood.

Mark: "Are you from the ship *Uranus*?" (The *Uranus* sank on May 10, 1887.)

Ghost Box: "Yes."

Norma: "Do you feel like you're lost?"

Ghost Box: "That's correct."

Norma: "How can we help you get home? How many are wandering here on the beach?"

Ghost Box: "Eight." "Three."

The two answers suggested that multiple groups of lost souls were nearby.

Norma: "Can you name one of the ships that sank here?"

Ghost Box: "John..." (but the rest was garbled).

Mark: "Are you the crew from the *John R. Williams*?"

To this question came an answer that may be one of the most remarkable responses from the afterlife ever recorded.

Ghost Box: "See us."

Norma: "Did I just hear 'see us'? Where can I see you? Where are you? Do you see us?"

Gerry began waving his arms to any possible nearby spirits. Norma continued monitoring.

Norma: "Do you see us waving?"

Ghost Box: "Yes."

Mark began waving his arms.

Gerry: "Are you standing on the sand?"

Norma: "Where are you?"

Ghost Box: "House."

Gerry: "Are you near the cement building?" (The nearby gun emplacement)

Ghost Box: "Yes."

Gerry: "Do you see me walking towards you?"

Gerry walked towards the cement bunker on the left when facing inland.

Ghost Box: "Yes." "Yes." "Yes." "Yes." "Yes."

Norma chuckled at all the responses. The excitement felt by the team was electric. *A spirit, or spirits, were beckoning us to come to them.* This *never* happens. It is always the investigator trying to coax the spirit to come to them for conversation. Plus, the length of the ongoing dialogue might have set a record. This was a first. Would we be able the see them in the daylight once we got to their location? Would there be handshaking all around? Or would everything dissipate once our energies and theirs mingle, as is the norm?

Mark and Norma began following Gerry towards the military bunker. Gerry reached the first level of dunes and was still waving towards the bunker. He was out of audio range for the recorder.

Norma: "Are we also heading in the same direction?"

Ghost Box: "Yes."

Norma: "Gerry is still waving. Do you still see him?"

Ghost Box: "Yes." "Yes."

Norma: "Gerry wants to know if he is close to you."

Ghost Box: "Yes. Close."

Norma: "Do you want him to stop where he's at, or keep going forward?"

The investigators were now at the top of the dunes, in front of the giant gun.

Norma: "Where do you want us to go?"

No answer.

Mark: "Can you still see Gerry waving?"

Ghost Box: "Yes."

Mark: "Are you at the top of the hill?"

Ghost Box: "Yes."

Mark: "Which hill? The closest hill, or the second hill?"

The dunes, like all dunes, had numerous small hills and valleys. Mark tried to clarify.

Mark: "Hill 'one' is closest to us, hill 'two' is the next, and hill 'three' is the farthest. Which one do you want us to be at?"

Ghost Box: "Three."

Mark: "We are coming up hill 'three'. Is that okay?"

We ground through the sand to the farthest hill.

Mark: "Can you still see us waving? Do you want us to stop at the top of this hill? Now we are at a fork at the top of hill 'three'. Do you want us to go left or right?"

Ghost Box: "Turn left."

Mark: "Is this were you want us to be? Do you still see us?"

Gerry: "How close are you to us now?"

Ghost Box: "Too close."

Gerry: "Too close! What does that mean?"

Ghost Box: "Hello."

Norma: "Hi!"

Norma said this as if talking to an old friend, then laughed.

Norma: "Do you know who I am?"

Mark: "Do you want us to be here, or keep walking towards the guns?"

Ghost box: "Keep walking. Please."

Norma suddenly realized a disturbing possibility.

Norma: "You're here in spirit. But are you trying to tell us where your physical body is?"

Ghost Box: "Yes. Us. Dead."

Their words came in quick succession.

Mark: "Is your physical body here on the beach?"

Ghost Box: "Physical. Death."

Mark: "Did you die on this beach? How many of you are here with us right now?"

Ghost Box: "Three."

Mark: "What ship are you on?"

Ghost Box: "Ship."

Norma: "So let's clarify. Is your physical body buried in this area?"

Ghost Box: "No."

Our anticipation lessened. It was a false alarm.

Misinterpreting dialogue between realms is easy to do. Often spirit-talk can lead down one road, then double back and head the opposite direction. Investigators are left confused. But then again, conversing across dimensions is a complex, iffy business on a good day. While ghosts and spirits see more than us, they are not infallible. They err. And some have a sense of humor. They may jerk you around for fun. That is what this event was beginning to feel like. When the ghost said "hello," it felt like we were right in front of it. Even Norma's "hi" sounded like she was talking to someone across the breakfast table.

Norma: "Was your body ever found? Were you given a proper burial?"

Ghost Box: "There were six of us fishing."

Ah, a fisherman — famous for fish stories.

Norma: "What was the name of your fishing boat? Why did you lead us to this location?"

No more answers were received. It was getting late and we needed to start for home. We were disappointed that we couldn't bring this important event to some conclusive result. It would have been nice to get people's names, and the correct name of their ship or boat. Take messages to descendants. Help with closure, something.

It wasn't meant to be.

Norma made the farewell.

Norma: "Thank you for your time. We'll review the tapes and we'll return if we can help you in any way. End session at 4:18 p.m."

Our next visit to Cape Henlopen State Park was Monday, Halloween Night, 2011. Norma could not attend. Mark and Gerry spent close to three hours on the beach, on a partly cloudy night with a quarter-moon, starting at 5:43 p.m. The temperature was between 47 and 55 degrees F., but the wind chill caused by 8 to 12 mph winds was around 40 degrees after the sun went down. We were facing the shore at 110 degrees east. EMF reading was zero. We parked on two beach chairs, with two umbrellas for a predicted downpour and various electronic items.

That night was the anniversary of the sinking of the *Kate Darling* which went down October 31, 1899. With stories of ghost ships and the dead walking on the beach, we felt that particular night would be the best time to witness something. The following snippet from the recorded report is a testimony to researchers everywhere who sacrifice hours of their lives for seconds of communication.

Fortunately, we didn't have to wait more than five minutes for something to happen.

Mark: "That was weird. Gerry, as I was just looking to my left, there was a shimmering wall of energy that moved in a wave towards the water. It was clear, but it distorted the horizon. It was long and about ten feet tall. It was like a clear sheet of energy rippling in the wind as it moved."

Gerry: (laughs) "A sheet? How appropriate on Halloween."

Mark directed his next question to ghost land.

Mark: "Was that you letting us know you are here?"

But there was no answer. Certainly any decent ghost would be out trick or treating. This incident happened about 5:54 p.m. with a still-bright sky. About twenty minutes later, Mark was listening for ghostly voices using a parabolic microphone. It sports a large plastic cone on the front to aid in capturing voices within 100 yards. It's used often during football games to catch the players' chatter. He was aiming it northward up the beach and clearly picked up the sound of a man talking about the weather. He didn't have my glasses with him, so when he looked, he *thought* he saw two people walking on the beach. They were, however, way out of the 100-yard range. They were close to 250-yards out.

Gerry: "There are two people down there and I picked up one of them talking."

Mark looked up the beach.

Mark: "You did? Isn't that wild. That microphone is only a forty-dollar toy version of the professional high-end ones."

But the joke was on Gerry. Later, when he was searching the area with the binoculars, he looked northward up the beach again and realized that he had *not* seen two people walking. He had been looking at two pilings that supported a large observation deck that sat above the beach. Mark confirmed this. Then we realized that since there had been no one walking on the beach; the voice heard must have been a spirit and would have been within the hundred-yard limit of the microphone. Perhaps it was a dead sailor still worried about sailing conditions.

It's funny how things come in threes. Less than a couple minutes after we realized the truth about the spirit talking of the weather, *more* voices were captured by the parabolic mic.

Gerry was aiming the mic almost directly southeast when two male voices were heard. Keep in mind the wind was smacking the device in a southerly way at about 10-12 mph. At times, this made quite a racket in the headphones. Despite that, the men's voices were clearly audible; they were speaking English, but sadly, perhaps due to the wind roar, Gerry couldn't determine the exact wording. The mic was in his right hand so he fast-jabbed Mark with his left to get his attention.

Mark: "What do ya got?"

Gerry tore the headphones off and shoved them at Mark, while trying to keep the microphone aimed at the exact spot where he had heard the voices. This was difficult while wearing insulated gloves and a winter coat, as the wind continued buffeting. It took Mark a precious few seconds to change headphones.

Gerry: "Do you hear it? Do you hear them?"

He was excited about another ghostly "hit" in so short a time. Maybe Halloween was the right night to be there.

Mark: "No."

Gerry: "There are people talking."

He insisted. They swapped equipment so Mark could take aim with the parabolic mic and try to reconnect with the conversation. But between coats, gloves, wind, the fear of dropping expensive electronics in the sand, and just plain clumsiness, by the time we were reset, the voices had ended.

The voices were from beach-combing specters. There was no one else around. From our beach chairs, looking southeast, we were only twenty-plus yards to the ocean, and from there the Atlantic was empty of ships and men out to the horizon.

The rest of the night sunk into war-time mode; hours of tedium broken by seconds of excitement. Despite constant monitoring of the beach with sweeps of the parabolic mic, no other voices were heard. We asked many questions to arouse response from despondent spirits, but we were ignored. Even the Ghost Box kept locking up. It was unusable. It felt like the majority of our time was wasting away. We began discussing UFOs, stars, constellations, everything but ghosts.

Then Mark turned to his left and fell silent.

Gerry: "Are you all right?"

Mark: "Do you see something reflecting on the side of this hill, about fifty yards in front of us?"

Gerry looked over his left shoulder. There was a white apparition elongated in a general human form, but without any specific features. It looked like a sheet! Moving away from us and up the dune, it was there about two seconds, then gone.

Gerry: "Yeah!"

Mark: "There's nothing out on the water that would cause that. It's a glowing object."

The sheet appeared again farther down the dunes. He then addressed the object.

Mark: "If that is someone standing over there, we can see you. Wave at us."

Gerry had retrieved the binoculars and was watching the glowing mass. It looked inhuman.

Mark: "Can you tell what it is?"

Gerry: "I cannot."

Gerry passed the binoculars to Mark.

Gerry: "See what you think. There is definitely something glowing. And do you see something standing in front of it?"

Mark: "There is something there. Now it's fading."

Gerry: "Let's go check it out. Grab the recorder and let's go."

After sitting on beach chairs for almost two hours, we were shockingly clumsy just getting to our feet, clutching microphones in arms, and tripping over the uneven sand. Unfortunately, we were in such a rush to get close to the glowing ghost that we forgot to take off our headphones. They were joined together with a splicer, and therefore, so were we.

Mark: "It's gone. We're still doing our due diligence by making sure it was not a reflection off a sign, because there is a sign right here."

The sign warned to stay off the dunes. It was about 9 x 16 inches of metal bolted to a seven-foot metal angle-iron that was sticking out of the sand.

Gerry: "No, no, it can't be that. It was a lot longer than that sign."

True. The first mist that we saw looked about six feet long.

Mark: "There it is again!"

Gerry: "Where, where?"

Mark: "I just saw a twinkle over there. I hope there are no lightning bugs out this time of year."

Gerry: "No way. They couldn't stand up to the wind."

Mark: "There it is again!"

Gerry: "Oh, over here!"

Mark: "Yeah, something just flashed at us."

We continued shuffling through the sand along the dunes, northward, trying to catch up with the spectral weirdo that was leading us farther from base.

Gerry: "There, it's over there! Why does it keep going further away?"

Mark: "I just saw it move!"

Gerry: "That's right. We're well past where we first saw it."

Mark: "Wait a minute, wait a minute. That's the metal sign!"

Gerry: "But the sign doesn't move."

We stared hard at the dunes to see what the hell was going on.

Gerry: "There! Just there! Did you see it?"

Mark: "No, I was looking…"

Gerry: "It keeps moving down the beach."

Mark: "Hold on. Are you sure it's not the signs? Here, back up."

We had been chasing the ghost close to the dune's boundary line. There were actually several warning signs spaced about twenty-yards apart. Now we stepped back towards the water for a bigger picture. As we turned to move back we noticed bright lights, two sets of two, out on the water.

Gerry: "What are those light out there?"

Pause

Mark: "Boats."

Mark's voice was droll, disappointed. We studied the lights for a couple of beats. The lights moved northward, away from us, at a slow pace.

Gerry: "All right. Let's walk backwards towards our base and see if the ships' lights bounce off the signs and create the same effect we've been following."

Backwards we went, watching for ghosts in front of us and sand piles, tire depressions, and driftwood behind us. All the while we would jerk each other's head back and forth via the short headphone wires.

Mark: "Look, it's doing it again right now. Do you see it?"

Gerry: "Yeah, that does look something like what we've been watching."

Mark: "That's got to be the explanation. Look, it's doing it again."

Damn. It would have been perfect to see something spooky on Halloween.

Gerry: "Okay, we chalk it up to the lights from the ships heading north, bouncing off the 'stay off the dunes' signs and reflecting the glowing figures on the dunes. I'm good with that."

Mark: "I'd rather know for sure. That's why we're here. Ghosts debunked."

Gerry: "We want the real, not the unreal."

No further paranormal events occurred on the beach. After about three hours of work, we packed up and trudged to the car about a half mile away, and headed back to Delaware City.

But the shoreline was not the only place where normal went awry that Halloween night.

Fort Miles, a single road with buildings and gun placements along each side.

The view looking out from within building T606, where the spirit of a private communicates with us from beyond.

Norma Forteza, ITC Research from the group PAST Intel is looking down at the ITC Device as we communicate with the spirits. Is there something standing behind her?

Gerry taking in the surroundings of the empty bunkhouse of building T606.

Gun placements that look out towards the ocean.

On the beach of Cape Henlopen during the
ITC Session, co-author Gerry Medvec and
investigator Norma Forteza.

Gerry checking his notes
as the spirits communicate
through the ITC Device.

The Mel-Meter (EMF and Type K thermo-coupler)
and the anemometer used to gather environmental
readings during the ITC session.

Gerry reviewing the
manifest of shipwrecks that
took place all up and down
the coast, from Rehobeth to
Cape Henlopen.

The dunes on Halloween, October 31, 2011; this is at the start of the Halloween investigation of the 112th anniversary of the shipwreck of *The Kate Darling*.

As dusk settles in on the Halloween Investigation, Gerry hears disembodied voices; this picture was taken at the moment he heard them and pointed to their origination.

Gerry is using the parabolic microphone with mono-scope as he looks down the beach in the direction where he heard the other voices calling out.

Gerry standing at the end of the barrel of one of the two massive guns that face the ocean from the side of the dunes.

Trickster in the Dénouement

From Gerry Medvec

What a blast it was sitting on the dark Cape Henlopen beach on Halloween night, hoping to view ghost ships, catch phantasms on film, and listen to the dead speak.

But the big event (for me) of that night occurred as we headed home to Delaware City. It was about 10:15 p.m. Mark was driving north on Route 1. We were about five miles south of Odessa (the highway sign we saw about a mile after the incident read: Odessa ...4 miles).

I dislike driving anymore. Because I'm getting old and crotchety? Not really. I enjoy the beauty of the American road: large fields, forests, grazing cattle, and river flows. Even at night, the dots of light from houses, street lamps, and refineries give the blackened landscape a Christmas feel throughout the calendar. As I gazed that night at the flat Delaware countryside, Mark and I discussed not only the ghostly voices on the Cape Henlopen beach, but also UFO topics for our upcoming co-authored book, *UFOs over Pennsylvania.* I was soon to be glad that I wasn't driving.

My contention is that alien probes visit this planet every night by the tens of thousands. I base this on the amount of probes I've seen at night in various parts of the country, without even trying: In California City, California; in Gettysburg and West Chester, Pennsylvania; and in Pine Bush, New York to note a few. The most numerous sightings I've had so far were in French Creek State Park, Elverson, Pennsylvania, where I counted fourteen probes in one night. Seven of them were scattered in different parts of the park, but seven others I saw were in the back yard of the house adjacent to the park's south entrance on Route 345. And I'll bet that the homeowners never had a clue the probes were out there. The people were probably watching TV or playing Wii. Meanwhile, devices from another world were floating outside their kitchen windows, unperturbed and undisturbed. They all glowed in a soft light that mimicked the exterior light on the back of the house. Up, down, back, forth, left and right, they moved in a constant jerky dance.

It is this constant shimmying that is one of the giveaways to their presence. Though human-made lights also appear to move in light-to-heavy winds, particularly when viewed through tree limbs, alien lights move even when all surrounding earth lights are still. Also, our lights have limited range, that is, the light doesn't shine through the fixture that is holding it. Alien lights have no fixture, no wires, nothing holding them. They float freely. And their globes emit light in all directions at once which backlights the globes themselves against any nearby earthly form.

All these observations and conclusions nearly flew in my face on Halloween Night, 2011.

As we drove on Route 1, we approached the overpass beneath which Route 13 slid. Straight out the passenger's window there was a private home with five or six smaller white buildings clustered loosely behind and left of the house. I could see that Willey's Produce was the next property on Route 13 going north.

One of the buildings had a large, bright exterior light hanging from a curved, stainless-steel lamp post above its roof. It gave off much bright light and illuminated most of the buildings and grounds around it. No more than ten to fifteen yards to the left of that light was another. Its color and intensity closely matched that of the light on the pole, so that, at a quick glance, you'd be hard pressed to tell they were from different manufacturers. But this second light shone in all directions and had no visible connection to anything. It simply floated in front of an evergreen tree.

Why would the owner put up two lights of identical intensity so close together, and string one of those heavy lights to hang in front of a tree?

He wouldn't.

It was an alien probe.

No sooner did I realize it was a probe, than it leapt into the air about thirty feet, came down in a perfect golden arch, like the hamburger logo, and stopped dead thirty to forty yards to its right (my left), hovering again at the same height it was at in its previous spot, about twenty-five feet up. This happened in *one second*.

"Whoa, whoa, whoa," was the best I could utter. I'd never seen alien globes do circus tricks before. What's more – I'd never had one *allow me to see it* spring into an arch like that! Did it think no one was watching? Or did it make a mistake? Did some other-worlder push the wrong control button? Could it have been intentional? Was it "show time?" Who else saw it?

Sadly, Mark's only experience was hearing me yell. By the time the probe did its big-top act, the homestead was slightly behind us out of his view.

The next day I returned to that Route 1 overpass. I parked there to see if there was a man-made light hanging in front of the evergreen tree and prove that I'd temporarily gone nuts the night before.

There was no light near the evergreen. The light on the lamp post was just where I'd seen it the night before. My mind was safe.

Every time I'd seen probe-globes in the past, they reacted in one of two ways. Though their light shines in every direction, it is brighter, more intense in the direction they are focused on: for instance, the ground. When I showed up, their intensity would change from the ground and swing around to "look" at me. The globe would then (usually) turn back to its original point of focus and ignore me.

Or...

...It would shoot off at unbelievable speed and return to the cosmos *in under a second*. Acceleration at that rate gives the appearance of disappearance. But it doesn't magically vanish. It leaves real fast – faster than we can see.

For whatever reason, this Halloween globe broke the pattern. It was a trick and a treat. Maybe it was just an error. Or perhaps they've come to terms with the idea that many of *us* know *they* are here.

Conclusion

I hope you've enjoyed the stories that we've presented here in this work. The paranormal is full of mysteries and unknowns, but through our collective experiences, we've begun to put together the pieces of this gigantic puzzle that has been at the root of the burning question that lives at the core of our existence: "What are ghosts?"

My experiences and my family's experiences are a part of this giant collective of shared experiences as a whole. These stories are just a glimpse of the reality that exists within our midst, but most of us choose not to see or be open to it. Take from them what you may, but understand that they are the sum part of greater answers to the question "What lies beyond?" that still eludes us. It is this drive and desire in me to understand that question and to know the answer that keeps my passion for investigating, writing, and helping others to understand these things.

The paranormal co-exists within our own reality, and these stories are just a glimpse of that reality that we all share.

Glossary of Terms and Definitions

The following Glossary section is provided by the Chester County Paranormal Research Society in Pennsylvania and appears in training materials for new investigators.

Please visit www.ChesterCountyprs.com for more information.

AIR PROBE THERMOMETER

A thermometer with an external probe that is capable of taking instant measurements of the air temperature.

ANOMALOUS FIELD

A field that can not be explained or ruled out by various possibilities, that can be a representation of spirit or paranormal energy present.

APPARITION

A transparent form of a human or animal, a spirit.

ARTIFICIAL FIELD

A field that is caused by electrical outlets, appliances, etc.

AURAL ENHANCER

A listening device that enhances or amplifies audio signals; i.e., Orbitor Bionic Ear.

AUTOMATIC WRITING

The act of a spirit guiding a human agent in writing a message that is brought through by the spirit.

BASE READINGS

The readings taken at the start of an investigation and are used as a means of comparing other readings taken later during the course of the investigation.

CLASSIC HAUNTING

See also "Residual Haunting."

DEMONIC HAUNTING

A haunting that is caused by an inhuman or subhuman energy or spirit.

DOWSING RODS

A pair of L-shaped rods, or a single Y-shaped rod, used to detect the presence of what the person using them is trying to find; i.e., spirits, water, other elements.

ELECTRO-STATIC GENERATOR

A device that electrically charges the air often used in paranormal investigations/research as a means to contribute to the materialization of paranormal or spiritual energy.

ELF

Extremely Low Frequency.

ELF METER/EMF METER

A device that measures electric and magnetic fields.

EMF

Electro Magnetic Field.

EVP

Electronic Voice Phenomena.

FALSE POSITIVE

Something that is being interpreted as paranormal within a picture or video and is, in fact, a natural occurrence or defect of the equipment used.

GAMERA

A 35mm film camera connected with a motion detector that is housed in a weather proof container and takes a picture when movement is detected. Made by Silver Creek Industries.

GEIGER COUNTER

A device that measures gamma and x-ray radiation.

GHOST BOX

A modified radio that allows for a constant sweep through the AM or FM frequency bands. This device is used as a means of real time communication with spirits or other intelligent entities, a.k.a. Hack Shack Box, ITC Radio, ITC Device.

HACK SHACK BOX

The same type of device as Ghost Box, but this device is the result of a modified Radio Shack branded AM/FM digital radio.

INFRA RED

An invisible band of radiation at the lower end of the visible light spectrum. With wavelengths from 750 nm to 1 mm, infrared starts at the end of the microwave spectrum and ends at the beginning of visible light. Infrared transmission typically requires an unobstructed line of sight between transmitter and receiver. Widely used in most audio and video remote controls, infrared transmission is also used for wireless connections between computer devices and a variety of detectors.

INTELLIGENT HAUNTING

A haunting of a spirit or other entity that has the ability to interact with the living and do things that can make its presence known.

ITC – "INSTRUMENTAL TRANS COMMUNICATION"

The means of communicating with intelligent spirits, ghosts, or dimensional beings with the use of a device – whether it's biological, mechanical, or electronic. ITC is the umbrella under which EVP, video feedback, mediumship, dowsing, scrying, and any other types of spirit communication fall.

MILLIGAUSS

Unit of measurement, measures in 1000th of a gauss and is named for the famous German mathematician, Karl Gauss.

ORBS

Anomalous spherical shapes that appear on video and still photography; commonly are false positives as the result of the proximity of the flash to the lens on the body of a camera; more often than not, they are dust particles or moisture that reflect the light from the flash.

PENDULUM

A pointed item that is hung on the end of a string or chain and is used as a means of contacting spirits. An individual will hold the item and let it hang from the finger tips. The individual will ask questions aloud and the pendulum answers by moving.

POLTERGEIST HAUNTING

A haunting that has two sides, but the same kinds of activity in common. Violent outbursts of activity with doors and windows slamming shut, items being thrown across a room and things being knocked off of surfaces. Poltergeist hauntings are usually focused around a specific individual who resides or works at the location of the activity reported, and, in some cases, when the person is not present at the location, activity does not occur. A poltergeist haunting may be the cause of a human agent or spirit/energy that may be present at the location.

PORTAL

An opening in the realm of the paranormal that is a gateway between one dimension and the next. A passageway for spirits to come and go through. See also Vortex.

RESIDUAL HAUNTING

A haunting that is an imprint of an event or person that plays itself out like a loop until the energy that causes it has burned itself out. *(Also called "Classic Haunting.")*

SCRYING

The act of eliciting information with the use of a pendulum from spirits.

TABLE TIPPING

A form of spirit communication, the act of a table being used as a form of contact. Individuals will sit around a table and lightly place there fingertips on the edge of the table and elicit contact with a spirit. The Spirit will respond by "tipping" or moving the table.

TALKING BOARDS

A board used as a means of communicating with a spirit. Also known as The Ouija Board.

VORTEX

A place or situation regarded as drawing into its center all that surrounds it.

WHITE NOISE

A random noise signal that has the same sound energy level found at all frequencies.

Equipment Explanations

In this section, the Chester County Paranormal Research Society looks at the application and benefits of equipment used on investigations with greater detail. The equipment used for an investigation plays a vital role in the ability to collect objective evidence and helps to determine what *is* and *is not* paranormal activity. But a key point to be made here is: The investigator is the most important tool on any investigation. With that said, let us now take a look at the main pieces of equipment used during an investigation...

THE GEIGER COUNTER

The Geiger counter is device that measures radiation. A "Geiger counter" usually contains a metal tube with a thin metal wire along its middle. The space in between them is sealed off and filled with a suitable gas, with the wire at about +1000 volts relative to the tube.

An ion or electron penetrating the tube (or an electron knocked out of the wall by x-rays or gamma rays) tears electrons off atoms in the gas. Because of the high positive voltage of the central wire, those electrons are then attracted to it. They gain energy that collide with atoms and release more electrons, until the process snowballs into an "avalanche," producing an easily detectable pulse of current. With a suitable filling gas, the flow of electricity stops by itself, or else the electrical circuitry can help stop it.

The instrument was called a "counter" because every particle passing it produced an identical pulse, allowing particles to be counted, usually electronically. But it did not tell anything about their identity or energy, except that they must have sufficient energy to penetrate the walls of the counter.

The Geiger counter is used in paranormal research to measure the background radiation at a location. The working theory in this field is that paranormal activity can affect the background radiation. In some cases, it will increase the radiation levels and in other cases it will decrease the levels.

DIGITAL AND 35MM FILM CAMERAS

The camera is an imperative piece of equipment that enables us to gather objective evidence during a case. Some of the best evidence presented from cases of paranormal activity over the years has been because of photographs taken. If you own your own digital camera or 35mm film camera, you need to be fully aware of what the cameras abilities and limitations are. Digital cameras have been at the center of great debate in the field of paranormal research over the years.

The earlier incarnations of digital cameras were full of inherent problems and notorious for creating "false positive" pictures. A "false positive" picture is a picture that has anomalous elements within the picture that are the result of a camera defect or other natural occurrence. There are many pictures scattered about the internet that claim to be of true paranormal activity, but in fact they are "false positives." Orbs, defined as anomalous paranormal energy that can show up as balls of light or streaks in still photography or video, are the most controversial pictures of paranormal energy in the field. There are so many theories (good and bad) about the origin of orbs and what they are. Every picture in the CCPRS collection that has an orb – or orbs – is not presented in a way that state that they are absolutely paranormal of nature. I have yet to capture an orb photo that made me feel certain that in fact it is of a paranormal nature.

If you use your own camera, understand that your camera is vital. I encourage all members who own their own cameras to do research on the make and model of the camera, and see what other consumers are saying about them. Does the manufacturer give any info regarding possible defects or design flaws with that particular model? Understanding your camera will help to rule out the possibility of interpreting a "false positive" for an authentic picture of paranormal activity.

VIDEO CAMERAS

The video camera is also a fundamental tool in the investigation as another way for collecting objective evidence that can support the proof of paranormal activity. The video camera can be used in various ways during the investigation. It can be set on a tripod and left in a location where paranormal activity has been reported. It can also be used as a handheld camera and the investigator will take it with them during their walk-through investigation as a means of documenting to hopefully capture anomalous activity on tape. Infra-Red technology has become a feature on most consumer-level video cameras, and, depending on the manufacturer, can be called "night shot" or "night alive." This technology allows us to use the camera in zero light. Most cameras with this feature will add a green tint or haze to the camera when it is being used in this mode. A video camera with this ability holds great appeal to the paranormal investigator.

EMF/ELF METERS

EMF=Electro Magnetic Frequency

ELF=Extremely Low Frequency

What is an EMF/ELF meter? Good question. The EMF/ELF meter is a meter that measures Electric and Magnetic fields in an AC or DC current field. It measures in a unit of measurement called "milligauss," named for the famous German mathematician, Karl Gauss. Most meters will measure in a range of 1-5 or 1-10 milligauss. The reason that EMF meters are used in paranormal research is because of the theory that a spirit or paranormal energy can add to the energy field when it is materializing or is present in a location. The theory says that, typically, an energy that measures between 3-7 milligauss may be of a paranormal origin. This doesn't mean that an artificial field can't also measure within this range. That is why we take base readings and make maps notating where artificial fields occur. The artificial fields are a direct result of electricity, i.e., wiring, appliances, light switches, electrical outlets, circuit breakers, high voltage power lines, sub-stations, etc.

The Earth emits a naturally occurring magnetic field all around it and has an effect on paranormal activity. Geo-magnetic storm activity can also have a great influence on paranormal activity. For more information on this kind of phenomena, visit: www.noaa.sec.com.

There are many different types of EMF meters; and each one, though it measures with the same unit of measurement, may react differently. An EMF meter can range from anywhere to $12.00 to $1,000 or more depending on the quality and features that it has. Most meters are measuring the AC (alternating current, the type of fields created by man-made electricity) fields and some can measure DC (direct current – naturally occurring fields. Batteries also fall into the category of DC) fields. The benefit of having a meter that can measure DC fields is that they will automatically filter out the artificial fields created by AC fields and can pick up more naturally occurring electromagnetic fields. Some of the higher-tech EMF meters are so sensitive that they can pick up the fields generated by living beings. The EMF meter was originally designed to measure the earth's magnetic fields and also to measure the fields created by electrical and artificial means.

There have been various studies over the years about the long term effects of individuals living in or near high fields. There has been much controversy as to whether or not long term exposure to high fields can lead to cancer. It has been proven though that no matter what, long term exposure to high fields can be harmful to your health. The ability to locate these high fields within a private residence or business is vital to the investigation. We may offer suggestions to the client as to possible solutions for dealing with high fields. The wiring in a home or business can greatly affect the possibility of high fields. If the wiring is old and/or not shielded correctly, it can emit high fields that may affect the ability to correctly notate any anomalous fields that may be present.

AUDIO RECORDING EQUIPMENT

Audio recording equipment is used for conducting EVP (Electronic Voice Phenomena) research and experiments. What is an EVP? An EVP is a phenomenon where paranormal voices or sounds can be captured with audio recording devices. The theory is that the activity will imprint directly onto the device or tape, but it has not been proven to be an absolute fact. The use of an external microphone is essential when conducting EVP experiments with analog recording equipment. The internal microphone on an analog tape recorder can pick up the background noise of the working parts within the tape recorder and can taint the evidence as a whole. Most digital recorders are quiet enough to use the internal microphone, but as a general rule of thumb, we do not use them. An external microphone will be used always. Another theory about EVP research is that an authentic EVP will happen below the range of 80 hertz. (Human voice range is typically 80 hertz – 1100 hertz.) This is a lower frequency range and isn't easily heard by the human ear, and the human voice does not emit in this range. EVP is rarely heard at the moment it happens – it is usually revealed during the playback and analysis portion of the investigation. With the recent surge in ITC devices, more and more EVPs are captured and heard in "real-time." The traditional EVP session is now referred to as a "passive" EVP session, as in most cases the EVP is not heard or caught until playback, after the session is over.

THERMOMETERS

The use of a thermometer in an investigation goes without saying. This is how we monitor the temperature changes during the course of an investigation. CCPRS is currently using digital thermometers with remote sensors as a way to set up a perimeter and to notate any changes in a stationary location of an investigation. The air-probe thermometer can take "real time" readings that are instantly accurate. This is the more appropriate thermometer for measuring air temperature and "cold spots" that may be caused by the presence of paranormal phenomena, but is not always the case. The IR (infra-red) non-contact thermometer is the most misused thermometer in the field of paranormal research. CCPRS does not own or use IR non-contact thermometers for this reason. The IR non-contact thermometer is meant for measuring surface temperatures from a remote location. It shoots an infrared beam out to an object, bounces to the unit, and gives the temperature reading. I have seen, first hand, investigators using this thermometer as a way to measure air temperature. NO, this is not correct! There is no practical use for an IR non-contact thermometer in paranormal investigating, unless you are specifically trying to measure the temperature of an object from a remote distance.

A Haunted Directory of Delaware

* It must be noted that some of the locations in this directory are listed here as a point of interest and reference, are privately owned businesses that are "open to the public." Those we've included in the book have page numbers; those that do not have page numbers are well-known haunted places in Delaware and we felt that it was worth giving them an "honorable mention" in this directory.

Any inquiries or interest in locations shown here should be pursued after the consent of the owner(s) has been given.

New Castle County

Newark, 94
Christiana Fire Co. Station 12
Cooches Bridge
Deer Park Inn and Tavern
Lums Pond State Park – Swamp Forrest Trail
Salem Church Road
The Valley – Pike Creek "Satan's House", 113
Wilmington, 37
Porky Oliver's Golf Course – Above Par, 51
Bellevue Hall Mansion
Dead President's Tavern
Rockwood Mansion
Bancroft Academy
New Castle, 26
Amstel House
David Finney Inn
Overview Gardens
Women's Correctional Institute
Delaware City, 54
Fort Delaware, 54
Polk Henry House, 62
Middletown – a centered history, 26
Locust Grove Farm – Middletown, 35

Kent County

Dover, 67
Garrison Lake – The Blue Coat Inn, 76
Dickinson Mansion, 77
The Governor's Mansion, 78
The Green at Dover, 79-81
Smyrna
Black Diamond Road – Black Diamond, DE, 82-83
North Union Street – Smyrna, 84

Sussex County

Cypress Swamp – Sussex County, 122
Southern Delaware, 125
Woonsocket – Mount Saint Charles Academy, 126
Frankford – Graveyard, 126
Fredrica – Highway 12 West,127
Seaford – Airport Road, 127-
Maggie's Bridge,
Shore Points
Cape Henlopen State Park,136
Bethany Beach
Addy Sea Inn
Lewes Beach
The Neighborhood of Bay Oaks

Ghost Towns of Delaware

Delaware is full of ghost towns, like most states. We were able to locate and visit several of these reported locations. They were not included in this book because there was not any paranormal activity reported or experienced. We did visit them and document them for future reference as part of our day excursions into southern Delaware and have provided two of these here as an additional point of interest.

NEW MARKET
New Market Church Cemetery – East Ellendale, DE

OWENS STATION
Owens Road and Beach Highway, Saint Johnston, DE

Resources

Websites used during the research of this book:

http://archives.delaware.gov

http://en.wikipedia.org/wiki/New_Castle_County,_Delaware - a history, Dover,DE history,

http://portal.delaware.gov/facts/history/delhist.shtml State of Delaware official
   site – history of DE

www.brainyquote.com/quotes/authors - various quotes

www.cityofnewarkde.us/index.aspx?NID=56 – history of Newark, DE

www.delawarecity.info/history.htm---history of Delaware City, DE

www.hsd.org/Delaware – Historical Society of Delaware – History of Delaware

www.middletownde.org/History-of-Middletown/ – Middletown history

www.rootsweb.ancestry.com/~dekent/history.htm – Kent Co. history

www.sussexcountyde.gov/about/history/ – Sussex Co.

www.udel.edu/anthro/decunzo/read/j.htm--history of New Castle city, DE

www.u-s-history.com/pages/h2279.html---Wilmington, DE

Notes

Notes